Nick Moseley

Nick Moseley was born in Trinidad in 1962, the son of a clergyman, and educated at Bristol Grammar School and Royal Holloway, University of London. He worked as an actor in the 1980s before entering the teaching profession in 1990. In 1997 he became Course Director of the BA (Hons) Acting programme at Italia Conti, where he began to develop his theories and training methodologies. Nick began teaching Meisner Technique in 2000. He is currently Principal Lecturer in Acting at The Royal Central School of Speech and Drama, where he has continued his Meisner teaching and research. His books *Acting and Reacting* and *Meisner in Practice* are also published by Nick Hern Books. He has three children and lives with his partner and family in Buckinghamshire.

Also by Nick Moseley

ACTING AND REACTING:
Tools for the Modern Actor

MEISNER IN PRACTICE:
A Guide for Actors, Directors and Teachers

ACTIONING
and How to Do It

NICK MOSELEY

NICK HERN BOOKS
London
www.nickhernbooks.co.uk

A *Nick Hern Book*

Actioning – and How to Do It
first published in Great Britain in 2016
by Nick Hern Books Limited, The Glasshouse,
49a Goldhawk Road, London W12 8QP

Designed and typeset by Nick Hern Books
Printed and bound in Great Britain by
Mimeo Ltd, Cambridgeshire PE29 6XX

A CIP catalogue record for this book is available
from the British Library

ISBN 978 1 84842 423 4

Woodland
CARBON
www.woodlandcarbon.co.uk
NICK HERN BOOKS
Printed on Carbon Captured paper

Contents

Introduction

The Actioning technique, sometimes called 'Psychophysical Actioning', is probably the most firmly established of all early rehearsal processes within the British theatre. Most drama schools and many directors see it as an essential part of rehearsal 'table work' and the bedrock of the actor's work on the text.

Contrary to popular belief, Actioning is not a Stanislavskian technique, and is in fact little used outside of the UK. It was devised and developed by the Joint Stock Theatre Company in the late 1970s under the direction of Bill Gaskill and Max Stafford-Clark, largely in order to empower the actor to serve the play and the production by making clear and simple choices on each line of the text. It has since found its way into the arsenal of the majority of UK actors and directors.

Put simply, the Actioning technique requires you, the actor, in the early stages of rehearsing a play, to divide up your own lines into separate phrases or thoughts, to assign each thought an 'action verb' which expresses the underlying intention of the line, and then, having assembled this series of verbs, to attempt to speak and act each thought in the manner of the chosen verb.

The verbs themselves must be 'transitive' – in other words, something your character can *do* to another character, such as 'prod', 'ridicule' or 'encourage', rather than non-transitive verbs such as 'muse', 'cry' or 'hesitate', which tend to pull your focus back onto yourself. This means that each thought, spoken with a particular action verb in mind, becomes an attempt to affect another character in the manner implied by that verb.

Actioning is radical because it always begins with the text itself, and with the creation of a 'template' of shifting character intentions that serves as a living analysis of the possible intentions of the playwright. The post-Stanislavskian technique of Active Analysis, by contrast, postpones engagement with the words of the text until the actor is physically and emotionally immersed in the imagined world of the play, and in the relationships and the journey of each scene. In Active Analysis actors initially *improvise* the dialogue of the play, exploring the relationships and the journey of each scene to the point where the actual text can be 'drip-fed' into the imaginary world thereby created.

There is much argument about which technique works better for actors, but for me the debate is largely irrelevant. In either case you are still faced with the problem of how you deal with that difficult moment when you have to start speaking words written by someone else, and possibly spoken by hundreds of actors before you, as if they had just spontaneously popped into your head within an entirely new and present situation!

My view is that the Actioning technique is a highly effective and efficient way of making the text your own from day one. By 'Actioning' the text, you can impose your actor's will upon it, not in a random or perverse way, but by applying an analytical process which encapsulates each moment of a play into a single word that you yourself have selected.

For Gaskill and Stafford-Clark, Actioning was partly a response to the difficulty their actors seemed to have with 'motivation', especially in the case of political and polemical texts. In productions such as David Hare's *Fanshen* (Joint Stock Theatre Company, 1975), some actors were apparently unable to find the impulse to speak and act in a way that would clearly and simply reveal the human story and the social narrative. The director required the actors to serve the production by inhabiting and 'living' the form of the text; by contrast the actors seemed to want to explore individualised subtextual narratives which were emotionally and psychologically complex but which blurred the dialectical storyline and disrupted its rhythm.

The beauty of the Actioning technique is that, from the outset, it demands that you (often in collaboration with your director) interrogate the text in minute detail in order to find the right verbs to express your interpretation of each thought. The choice of a single verb, simple though it might seem, requires you to think about character, situation, scene objective and relationships at each point in the text, and to encapsulate them in one word. Having chosen your verbs, you then also have to 'play' them, through clear and tangible vocal shifts between one verb and the next. By bringing your vocal and physical resources to the task of delivering a line in the manner of the verb, you then start to own the text from a very early stage of rehearsal.

Actioning has often been criticised for being 'inorganic', and for not allowing the actor enough space to discover the meaning of the text through rehearsal and interaction. Actors have claimed to feel 'straitjacketed' and constricted by their action-verb choices, unable to speak as their impulse dictates in the moment. My view of this is that Actioning is no different from any of the other 'set' elements of the play and production. You cannot generally stray from the playwright's text, or from the moves set by the director, since those elements are fixed. So it is with the action verbs, yet none of these fixed aspects necessarily leads to a fixed performance. Even within those boundaries, you, the actor, still have huge scope for being reactive, impulsive and present, and no two performances will ever be quite the same. Like the text, the blocking and all the other fixed elements of a performance, the action verbs are there to help and support you – to give you a structure and a direction so that you can be free to respond in the moment without fear of losing the thread of the narrative or the form of the play.

Having said that, it is important to remember that action verbs can also be changed, not randomly or inadvertently, but through moments of clarity and realisation, when you decide at some point in rehearsal that your initial choice is not working. My view is that you are more likely to arrive at such moments by making clear and definite choices to begin with.

It might also be argued that Actioning serves another vital purpose, crucial to the age we live in, which is to force actors to develop vocal and physical precision and to broaden their expressive range, in a world where so much of our communication is now electronic – and where the notion of being physically, vocally and mentally 'present' is blurred by the reality that, for much of our lives, we are communicating simultaneously within two or three different contexts. For young actors in particular, the process of turning the body into a clear and efficient signifier, and of focusing the mind onto a single thought and intention in each moment of the action, works in opposition to the recent cultural shifts which encourage a much more dispersed energy and divided focus. This is not an entirely new endeavour – actors have always had to learn to speak and move with clarity – but there has never been a greater need for core training techniques which inspire and stimulate actors to expand and refine their physical and vocal capacity. Actioning is such a technique, and I believe it to be a fundamental tool for approaching text.

This book will attempt to go beyond traditional notions of using Actioning in rehearsal, by investigating the Actioning technique both as a tool for analysing and speaking text, and as a springboard into the actual staging of a scene. When I first used the technique, as an actor in the 1980s, I found it hard to see the connection between the action verbs chosen on the text and the work done on the rehearsal-room floor, and I saw other actors also struggling with this. Over many years of teaching the technique I have realised that action verbs also have a strong spatial/physical dimension which offers the actor possibilities for interacting with other characters and with the space. In the later chapters of this book I will be giving an account of these discoveries and showing how the actor can use Actioning as a physical as well as a verbal tool.

Acknowledgements

Max Stafford-Clark for allowing me to interview him about the Actioning technique.

The students of the BA (Hons) Acting Course at The Royal Central School of Speech and Drama for helping me explore these ideas over a number of years.

My partner for her tolerance and support.

1

*Beginning
Actioning*

The aim of this chapter is to help you develop skills in the first stages of the Actioning technique, namely the *analysis of the text* preparatory to *choosing your action verbs*. We need to be clear from the outset that Actioning is in no sense an alternative to other text work which an actor undertakes. It is impossible, in fact, to 'action' a text effectively without having first undertaken a range of Stanislavsky-derived processes and exercises, in order to establish, as appropriate, the background context and the specific circumstances in which a scene takes place. This analysis is a lengthy process in itself, but for the purposes of this chapter I have provided, in condensed form, much of the information you will need to get started on Actioning the sample texts and scenes.

As you will see, the business of choosing action verbs is not mechanical or formulaic. Rather it requires the actor to enter into a 'dialogue' with the text in order to tease out the right verbs. A great deal of analysis and thought has to go into this process, but the need to arrive at a *single verb* for each thought within the text stops this dialogue from turning into 'psychobabble' and saves the actors from drowning in a sea of possibilities. It is essential that when you first get up to rehearse a scene, you are only playing one choice at a time!

1

The sample dialogue below is designed to illustrate on a simple level some of the key features you will later identify in more complex scripts.

Sample Dialogue 1

(UNIT 1)

A newsagent's shop. BECKY (aged eighteen) is standing behind the counter, checking off something on a list. JOHN enters the shop. BECKY looks up.

JOHN. Hi. / Could I get some headache pills?

   BECKY *looks behind her at the row of medications.*

BECKY. Which sort?

JOHN. Have you got any paracetamol?

BECKY. No, sorry, / just Nurofen and Anadin.

JOHN. Okay then, could I have some Nurofen?

_____EVENT_____

(UNIT 2)

BECKY. Are you over sixteen? / I'm not allowed to sell them otherwise.

JOHN. Of course I am.

BECKY. Do you have any ID?

JOHN. No, I didn't bring any. / Look, this is crazy, I'm twenty-two!

BECKY. You don't look it.

JOHN. Come on, take a look at me. / Do I really look fifteen?

BECKY. I could get into trouble.

JOHN. Trust me, I'm twenty-two!

BECKY (*doubtfully*). Okay.

   She hands him the Nurofen.

The analysis of any scene, be it simple or complex, must always begin with the following questions:

1

1. What are the broad given circumstances? Include era, location, season, time of day, specific setting.

2. What are the specific given circumstances? Include characters and their backstories; previous relationships, if any; the basic contention (what the scene is about).

3. What do the characters *want*? We call these 'wants' objectives. Whose objective is the strongest? This person will be the scene driver.

4. What is stopping each character achieving their objective? This is the obstacle. Obstacles are usually created by the resistance of the other character.

5. What events happen in the scene, which change the situation? An event signifies the start of a new unit within the text.

6. What are the smaller 'wants' – sub-objectives – within each unit, which are leading towards the bigger want – main objective?

7. Are there any counter-objectives? A counter-objective is *something else* the character wants, or wants to avoid, which is in some measure opposed to the main objective, so that it becomes an internal obstacle.

Since the two characters in this scene clearly do not know each other, and the nature of their encounter is largely transactional, the given circumstances of the scene are relatively straightforward, as are the character objectives. John (the scene driver) clearly has a

1

main objective 'to buy tablets to cure his headache'. In the first unit of the scene, his sub-objective might be 'to find out what tablets they have in the shop'. There is no serious obstacle to this, and he 'caps' this objective easily.

An event then takes place, in which Becky, who has presumably been focusing mainly on the shelves up until that point, suddenly realises that John looks very young. This creates a new unit, and although John's main objective does not change, his sub-objective now becomes 'to convince Becky of his age'. His obstacle is now Becky's doubt.

Becky's main objective is probably 'to do her job properly'. In the first unit her sub-objective might be 'to assist John', while in the second unit she perhaps wants 'to be sure John is over sixteen' because she feels her job might be at risk. She has no significant obstacle in the first unit (other than the absence of paracetamol), but in the second unit, her obstacle is that John has no ID. Becky also has a counter-objective, which is that she doesn't want to annoy a customer, as this could also have consequences for her. This puts her into a dilemma, which requires John's help to be resolved.

Once you have considered all of these questions, and before you can 'action' the text, you next have to divide the dialogue into 'thoughts', as indicated by the forward slashes in the text above. Some speeches will just be a single thought; others will contain several 'thought-changes'. Broadly, the definition of a thought is *the extent of what a character intended to say when they started speaking*. That may be just a short phrase

1

or sentence, or it may be several lines. The new thought begins when the character suddenly thinks of something new, or additional, to say, or when another character starts to speak. Each thought will have its own action verb allocated to it.

John's first line is divided into two thoughts. 'Hi' is clearly just a conventional greeting, and the verb we allocate will probably be I GREET. The intention of this action is presumably to get Becky's attention in a friendly way. His second thought, 'Could I get some headache pills?', although framed as a question, is in fact quite an urgent request, so I SOLICIT might be the verb. The verb reflects the level of need, which we can assume is fairly acute.

Becky's first thought – 'Which sort?' – is a simple I QUESTION, as is John's reply 'Have you got any parac-etamol?', although in this context we might use I PROBE, reflecting the level of need. Becky's 'No, sorry' is clearly I PLACATE, while her 'Just Nurofen and Anadin.' might be I CHEER. Note that we are focusing on Becky's *intention*, not the actual *effect* of the infor-mation on John. John might, for example, be disappointed by the news that there is no paracetamol, but Becky's action is not I DISAPPOINT because that is not the *intended effect*.

It is worth mentioning at this point that when you choose your action verbs, you should as far as possi-ble avoid 'neutral' verbs like 'I INFORM'. The reason for this is that verbs of this kind don't really suggest a strong intention or strategy, and consequently they do not offer the actor a clear instruction about how to speak or move. The short scene above might not seem particularly exciting, yet however seemingly dull the dialogue, it is the actor's job to reveal the dramatic action through the action choices. A headache might not seem to be the most dramatic premise for a scene, but it is never the actor's job to downplay the central issue. As we know, quite small things can seem very important to those actually in the situation!

John's next line 'Okay then, could I have some Nurofen?' is probably I INSTRUCT, even though it is phrased as a question. This should really end the transaction and cap both objectives, but at this point the EVENT happens. Becky notices that John appears to be quite young, and she is suddenly thrown into doubt about whether she is allowed to proceed with the transaction. Her first thought is 'Are you over sixteen?' (I QUIZ), followed by 'I'm not allowed to sell them otherwise' for which you might choose I EDUCATE. (Again, we avoid I INFORM.) The reason we choose this verb is that Becky first asks a question but doesn't wait for the answer. From this we can infer that she sees a reaction arising in John (possibly confusion about why she has asked his age) and seeks to anticipate it.

John's answer 'Of course I am' indicates that he thinks this a stupid and unnecessary question. I would choose I RIDICULE as an action for this thought, which may seem a strong choice, but when choosing action verbs you have to take into account the precise circumstances. In this case, John, with a severe headache, has had to accept his second choice of medication, and is now faced with the possibility of not being allowed to buy it at all. For him this is a highly problematic situation, and he reacts accordingly. As a general rule I would always encourage actors to pick stronger rather than weaker verbs, because strong verbs force actors to engage with each other and discover the contention of a scene.

Becky's reply 'Have you got any ID?' may seem quite provocative, but it is likely that her only intention here is to INVITE him to present his ID so that they can both move on. John then REJECTS her invitation ('No, I didn't bring any') and proceeds to UNDERMINE her ('Look, this is crazy, I'm twenty-two'). Becky counters with 'You don't look it' (I RESIST). John presumably realises that he does look younger than his age, but since he does not have to prove his actual age, merely that he is over sixteen, he CHALLENGES her ('Come on, take a look at me') and then INTERROGATES her ('Do I really look fifteen?').

Becky then APPEALS TO him with her line 'I could get into trouble', upon which he REASSURES her with 'Trust me, I'm twenty-two'. Finally she ACCEPTS him ('Okay'), the transaction takes place, he caps his objective, and the scene ends.

The key to choosing verbs that are both accurate and stimulating lies in the actors' ability to bring the text to life in their imagination. Thoughts should never be considered out of context, but should always be seen as part of the through-line of the dialogue. Imagining how the dialogue might *sound* will also encourage you to choose strong and evocative verbs, rather than neutral or uninspiring ones. Strong verbs are not only easier to relate to and play; they are also far more likely to stimulate a reaction from your fellow actor once you start to get a scene onto its feet.

1

I should also emphasise that the verb choices listed above are not the only possibilities. You may have your own suggestions or interpretations that give you a clearer sense of the action, or even lead you to play a thought differently. The initial verb choices are merely 'ways in' to the scene. They stop you getting stuck in flat and meaningless delivery of the text when you start rehearsing, and they help you realise the different moments and shifts within the scene. Many of the action verbs you choose will remain throughout rehearsal, but some may change as you gain a deeper understanding of a scene and take account of your fellow actors' choices. For this reason, all action verbs (and indeed all text notes) should be written in pencil!

The second excerpt, below, requires you to consider not just the dialogue itself, but the background circumstances and the backstories of both characters:

Sample Dialogue 2

The given circumstances are that Sam, who has no money and lots of debts, has managed to borrow two hundred pounds from Rosie, an ex-girlfriend who lived with him in the flat for two years, and with whom he is still on very good terms. His current girlfriend, Fran, is suspicious of Rosie, who is not just Sam's ex but also his childhood friend. The previous evening Sam arrived home quite drunk, thinking the money was in his jacket pocket, but he now can't find it.

A shabby shared living room in a rented flat. Sunday morning.
A battered black-leather sofa and two mismatched armchairs.
Mess, beer cans, rubbish. SAM (late twenties) dressed only in

T-shirt and boxer shorts, is looking for something. He searches among the rubbish, then stops and thinks. The doorbell rings.

_____EVENT FOR SAM_____

SAM *answers it. It is* FRAN, SAM's *girlfriend (early twenties).*

FRAN. Morning!

SAM. Hi.

   FRAN *steps into the flat and stares around with distaste.*

FRAN. This place is a tip. / You should clear it up.

SAM. Why don't *you?* (*He resumes searching.*)

_____EVENT FOR FRAN_____

FRAN. It's not my flat. / Looking for something?

_____EVENT FOR SAM_____

SAM. Nothing important.

FRAN. If it wasn't so messy you wouldn't lose things.

SAM. Yeah thanks for that.

FRAN. What you lost?

SAM. Nothing.

FRAN. Must be something.

SAM. Just some money.

FRAN. Money? / How much money?

SAM. Just some money, okay?

FRAN. What money?

SAM. It's a loan.

FRAN. A loan? / Who from?

SAM (*after a pause*). Rosie.

Objectives and Given Circumstances

Although some of the action verbs within this dialogue might be fairly obvious, others will require a working knowledge of the play's given circumstances, and an understanding of the characters' objectives. Words on a page can be deceptive, and it is all too easy to mistake

1

the intention of the character if you are unclear about the situation.

In this case we need to start from the given circumstances and decide on objectives for the characters. We know that Fran is insecure about Rosie, not least because Rosie cohabited with Sam, which Fran doesn't yet. From this we can surmise that Fran's main objective might be 'to be a bigger part of Sam's life'. Sam's main objective, on the other hand, is more likely to be 'to stop everything falling apart'. Within the excerpt itself, however, Fran has two sub-objectives. At the start she wants Sam to tidy the flat; soon after, however, she wants to find out about the money. Sam also has two sub-objectives. He starts off wanting to find the money, and then wants to avoid a row about Rosie. You will notice that each of the sub-objectives connects back to the character's main objective.

Other given circumstances include the fact that Sam has been out without Fran the previous night. He has implied to her that this was with male friends, without revealing to her that Rosie was one of the group.

Fran's opening action 'Morning!' looks like a fairly obvious I GREET, yet in the context of Sam's state of dishevelment, it might be I TEASE, which gets the scene off to a clearer start. Sam's 'Hi' could also be I GREET, but here again you could make a more interesting choice. In Sam's eyes this is not a good time for Fran to call, especially in such a cheery mood. It might be better to choose I FREEZE for this thought. Fran's next action 'This place is a tip' is a fairly obvious I CHASTISE, as is her second action I GALVANISE ('You should clear it up'). Sam's response 'Why don't *you*?'

12

could be I SILENCE. It is clear that Fran has previously criticised the state of the flat, and Sam does not want to have the argument again. Fran then changes tack, reminding him that she doesn't live with him and therefore cannot take responsibility: 'It's not my flat' – I REMIND. She then becomes aware of what Sam is doing, and her next thought 'Looking for something?' is probably I QUESTION. At this point it is necessary for anyone Actioning Sam's lines to know the given circumstances, since his reply 'Nothing important' could easily be interpreted as carrying an action like I REASSURE. However, the given circumstances tell us that Sam is feeling guilty about borrowing money from Rosie, which means the action on that line is more likely to be I DIVERT or I BLOCK. It is also likely that Sam, realising that Fran is curious about his search, will stop looking for the money at this point in order not to arouse further curiosity, although the need to find it will remain strong.

As it happens, Fran is still concerned with her first sub-objective, which is to get Sam to clean up the flat, and she takes the opportunity to push this further: Fran's line 'If it wasn't so messy you wouldn't lose things' might be I CRITICISE or I SCOLD. Sam's response, 'Yeah, thanks for that' is reminding her that such comments are not helpful, therefore I REBUKE is probably the action verb.

Unfortunately it works too well, because by once more silencing Fran on the subject of the messy flat, Sam shifts her focus back onto the lost item. 'What you lost?' could be I PROBE, which Sam counters with 'Nothing' – I EVADE. 'Must be something' is I PURSUE, upon which Sam realises she is too interested and he has to tell her something. 'Just some money' is I PLACATE, although unfortunately Fran is far from placated. 'Money?' has to be similar to I PURSUE but stronger.

This is something you will encounter fairly frequently within your Actioning work – a series of actions, which are essentially all doing the same thing, only with increasing intensity. Your job is to find a series of verbs that reflect this. For 'Money?' I would suggest I PRESS, and for 'How much money?' I INTERROGATE.

Sam then DISMISSES with 'Just some money, okay?', upon which Fran ups the stakes and comes back with 'What money?' (I SHAKE). Sam gives in to this, and says 'It's a loan' (I SATISFY). Fran, however, is far from satisfied, but since he is no longer avoiding giving her an answer, she can afford to play the gentler actions I QUERY on 'A loan?' and I QUIZ on 'Who from?' This of course is the one thing Sam doesn't want to tell her – his objective is to stop things falling apart, which may well happen if Fran decides that Rosie is too prominent in his life. However, he realises that to lie to her would probably make things even worse, so reluctantly he admits 'Rosie' on the action verb I SUBMIT TO (we add the preposition to make the verb transitive).

The business of Actioning always has to start from the assumption that there are no 'throwaway' lines in dramatic text, and that every line is driven by a character intention. In most scenes, many of the action verbs will be fairly obvious. However, without knowledge of the given circumstances and objectives you can easily miss the subtextual tension in the scene, which might lead you to choose weaker and less interesting verbs. In later chapters we will investigate how the actor uses the verbs he has chosen to get to the heart of the action and discover the 'shape' of the scene.

1

2

*Complex
Text*

The two scenes we have looked at in the previous chapter are relatively simple in terms of the characters' backstories and the social conventions which influence them. However, many plays, especially those from different eras/places from your own, can present you with difficulties when it comes to choosing the right verbs.

The excerpt below is from Act One of *The Importance of Being Earnest* by Oscar Wilde. I have chosen this play because, although it is a 'well-made' piece with boldly drawn characters and a clear 'arc' to the story, it has a complex plot involving a great deal of deception and subterfuge. This means that the characters' real intentions are often hidden below the frothy, witty dialogue, requiring you, the actor, to do plenty of investigation before you start to 'action' the scene.

The scene is the London apartment of Algernon Moncrieff, a young aristocratic man-about-town of the 1890s. Algernon's friend Jack Worthing, under his customary pseudonym of Ernest, has come up to London from his Hertfordshire estate in order to propose to Gwendolen Fairfax, daughter of Lord and Lady Bracknell, and Algernon's cousin. Algernon considers Jack (whom he knows as Ernest) to be too serious, but since he has very little income of his own and Jack is quite wealthy, Algernon cultivates his friendship. Algernon is also very interested in Jack's other life in the country, about which Jack will say nothing. This interest has been compounded by the fact that on a previous visit, Jack left behind a cigarette case inscribed 'From little Cecily, with her fondest love to her dear Uncle Jack'. Cecily is in fact Jack's eighteen-year-old ward, the granddaughter of his late guardian and benefactor. Algernon correctly guesses that Cecily is young and attractive, and is determined to meet her.

Sample Dialogue 3

From very near the beginning of the play.

> ALGERNON. How are you, my dear Ernest? / What brings you up to town?
>
> JACK. Oh, pleasure, pleasure! / What else should bring one anywhere? / Eating as usual, I see, Algy!
>
> ALGERNON (*stiffly*). I believe it is customary in good society to take some slight refreshment at five o'clock. / Where have you been since last Thursday?
>
> JACK (*sitting down on the sofa*). In the country.
>
> ALGERNON. What on earth do you do there?
>
> JACK (*pulling off his gloves*). When one is in town one amuses oneself. When one is in the country one amuses other people. / It is excessively boring.
>
> ALGERNON. And who are the people you amuse?
>
> JACK (*airily*). Oh, neighbours, neighbours.
>
> ALGERNON. Got nice neighbours in your part of Shropshire?
>
> JACK. Perfectly horrid! Never speak to one of them.
>
> ALGERNON. How immensely you must amuse them! / (*Goes over and takes sandwich.*) By the way, Shropshire is your county, is it not?

JACK. Eh? Shropshire? / Yes, of course. / Hallo! / Why all these cups? / Why cucumber sandwiches? / Why such reckless extravagance in one so young? / Who is coming to tea?

ALGERNON. **Oh! merely Aunt Augusta and Gwendolen.**

_____**EVENT FOR JACK**_____

JACK. How perfectly delightful!

ALGERNON. Yes, that is all very well; but I am afraid Aunt Augusta won't quite approve of your being here.

JACK. May I ask why?

ALGERNON. My dear fellow, the way you flirt with Gwendolen is perfectly disgraceful. / It is almost as bad as the way Gwendolen flirts with you.

JACK. I am in love with Gwendolen. / **I have come up to town expressly to propose to her.**

_____**EVENT FOR ALGERNON**_____

ALGERNON. I thought you had come up for pleasure? / ...I call that business.

JACK. How utterly unromantic you are!

ALGERNON. I really don't see anything romantic in proposing. / It is very romantic to be in love. / But there is nothing romantic about a definite proposal. / Why, one may be accepted. / One usually is, I believe. / Then the excitement is all over. / The very essence of romance is uncertainty. / If ever I get married, I'll certainly try to forget the fact.

Your first job, having read and re-read the text you are planning to 'action', is to start to delve below the surface of the dialogue, using Stanislavskian processes to reveal the detail of the situation and the motivating factors. (In most productions you will probably do this as a company, during the early stages of rehearsal.)

Superficially, this dialogue appears to be little more than a witty exchange between two leisured and slightly languid young men, and, sadly, it is all too often played as such. Hidden beneath the wit, however, is a mutual suspicion, and a need on the part of both men (for different reasons) to thwart each other's designs.

As with most scenes, it is impossible to make useful and accurate action-verb choices without a full understanding of the play's given circumstances. As a general principle, before attempting to 'action' a scene like this, you will need to:

- Read the whole play carefully at least twice, even if you are only Actioning one or two scenes, until you are absolutely clear about the plot, and have 'sifted' the text for information about the characters.

- Research the context, including the social structure, social and moral codes and any other relevant information about upper-class life of the time.

- Investigate and write down the given circumstances, in this case paying particular attention to the plot information offered through the course of Act One.

- Make yourself very familiar with all the characters and relationships, and the sequence of events. You may wish to construct charts and timelines to help you do this.

- Construct an actor's notebook. This will usually be a bound notebook with a hard cover, in which you write or insert all your notes and research. You should also cut and paste your script, page by page, into the notebook, leaving a blank page opposite each page of text for notes and annotations.

- Within the text itself, note down the key events as they occur in the dialogue. Events can be the entrance or exit of a character, or a revelation by one character to another. In the dialogue above (marked in bold) the main events are Algernon's revelation to Jack that Lady Bracknell and Gwendolen are expected, and Jack's revelation to Algernon that he is intending to propose to Gwendolen. Events often change the energy and pace of a scene, and also alter the sub-objectives (the smaller objectives which lead to the bigger ones). An event signals the start of a new unit.

Below is an example of a chart of character circumstances. Here I have noted down the background information and motivating forces for the four main characters, using a mixture of fact and conjecture to build a picture which can stimulate the imagination of the actor, but is at the same time carefully rooted in the actual given circumstances. (There are many more characters in the play, and many more plot twists that you would also have to investigate were you to 'action' the whole play.)

2

2

Jack (Ernest) Worthing	A foundling, discovered in a leather handbag (a kind of holdall rather than a ladies' handbag) at Victoria Station by Thomas Cardew, a rich elderly gentleman who subsequently adopted him. Now a young man in his twenties with a large income and nothing particular to do with his time, he has been given responsibility for looking after Cecily Cardew, granddaughter of his late guardian, a task which he has taken very seriously. However, as Cecily has approached adulthood, Jack has felt the need to spend time in London rather than with Cecily on his sleepy Hertfordshire estate with neighbours he hates. He has therefore invented a fictional younger brother, Ernest, who lives in London and constantly gets into scrapes from which he needs rescuing. Once in London, he takes the name of Ernest himself, in order to enjoy himself in the flamboyant society of his friend Algernon and others. He conceals from Algernon the true whereabouts of his country estate, claiming to live nearly two hundred miles away in Shropshire.
	Recently he has fallen in love with Gwendolen Fairfax, daughter of Lord and Lady Bracknell, and Algernon's cousin. This presents him with all sorts of difficulties, since once engaged he will no longer be able to keep his two lives separate. His feelings compel him to propose to Gwendolen, but he has no real plan beyond that, other than concealing from both Algernon and Gwendolen (for different reasons) that he has a very pretty young ward.
Algernon Moncrieff	The son of an army general and the nephew of Lady Bracknell. Although from aristocratic stock he has little income of his own, and lives on his debts. A flamboyant good-timer, he takes very little in life seriously. He values his freedom and often leaves London on exploratory jaunts, having invented an invalid friend called Bunbury whom he always claims to be visiting. Recently he has travelled all over Shropshire hunting for Jack's estate and is now convinced that Jack has been lying to him. His interest in Jack's private life has recently been exacerbated by the fact that Jack (whom he knows only as Ernest) has recently left behind in the apartment a silver cigarette case inscribed with the words 'From little Cecily with fondest love to her dear Uncle Jack'. At the start of the play he is already in love with the idea of Cecily and is determined to find out who she is.

Gwendolen Fairfax	A self-assured debutante, seeking marriage at least partly as an escape from her domineering mother, Lady Bracknell. Sees Jack (Ernest) as the ideal partner, being rich, good-looking and completely malleable.
Cecily Pardew	An unspoiled yet wealthy eighteen-year-old living relatively simply on Jack's country estate, bored with her elderly governess, Miss Prism, and secretly in love with Jack's wayward (and non-existent) brother Ernest, to whom in her fantasy she has already become engaged.

2

Objectives

Having established all the background and plot information, you will need to make some initial choices about what each character *wants* during the scene, and what you feel their major obstacle is. Sometimes it is useful to start with the super-objective of the play. The super-objective can be defined as the fundamental 'want' of the play. It is the principal driver of the action, powered from a basic 'lack' that motivates and inspires the main protagonists to pursue their specific objectives.

In this case each protagonist lacks a marital partner, which makes the super-objective of the play 'I want to get married'. (Six out of the seven major characters in this play carry this super-objective, while the seventh character, Lady Bracknell – who is married already – acts as antagonist, obstructing or disapproving of each match.)

Having articulated the super-objective, you can work down to the characters' main objectives and then to the scene objectives, as follows:

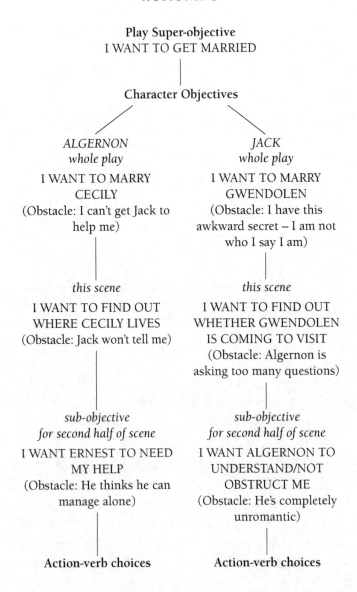

Play Super-objective
I WANT TO GET MARRIED

Character Objectives

ALGERNON
whole play
I WANT TO MARRY
CECILY
(Obstacle: I can't get Jack to
help me)

JACK
whole play
I WANT TO MARRY
GWENDOLEN
(Obstacle: I have this
awkward secret – I am not
who I say I am)

this scene
I WANT TO FIND OUT
WHERE CECILY LIVES
(Obstacle: Jack won't tell me)

this scene
I WANT TO FIND OUT
WHETHER GWENDOLEN
IS COMING TO VISIT
(Obstacle: Algernon is
asking too many questions)

sub-objective
for second half of scene
I WANT ERNEST TO NEED
MY HELP
(Obstacle: He thinks he can
manage alone)

sub-objective
for second half of scene
I WANT ALGERNON TO
UNDERSTAND/NOT
OBSTRUCT ME
(Obstacle: He's completely
unromantic)

Action-verb choices

Action-verb choices

A quick look at these objectives and obstacles reveals that, despite being friends and enjoying witty aphoristic banter, Jack and Algernon are in fact each other's foil and obstacle. Their conflict arises from the fact that Jack is participating in London's high society under an alias, and does not trust Algernon either to keep his secret or to stay away from Jack's ward, Cecily.

Choosing Your Action Verbs

2

Armed with all this information, you should now be in a position to go back to the scene itself and start speculating about your character's intention on each line. What effect do they wish to have on the other character? How are they responding to what has just happened? And what single verb seems to sum up that intention? To make effective action-verb choices you will need to analyse each moment within this conflict, and track the characters' shifting thoughts as they seek to outmanoeuvre each other.

You now proceed to make your action-verb choices and to write them down. This may sound simple, and for some thoughts the action verbs will be fairly obvious. At other times a level of analysis and subtextual investigation may be required to make the right choices. This analysis is essential to Actioning, because the verbs you choose will ultimately affect not just how you speak the text, but how you think and move, and how your character perceives other characters.

One of problems you might experience when you start Actioning is not being able to think of the right verb, even if you are fairly sure what the nature of the action is. If you are a newcomer to this technique, it is probably a good idea to obtain a list or book of action verbs which you can consult as you go along. The most commonly consulted volume, and the one I would recommend, is *Actions: The Actors' Thesaurus* by Marina

Caldarone and Maggie Lloyd-Williams (Nick Hern Books, 2004), which is also now available as an app for iOS devices. You might also find it useful to consult a standard thesaurus of synonyms and antonyms, either in book form or online.

Once you have actioned a few texts you will probably be able to identify the right verbs more easily, but for now, use whatever assistance you can find, which may also include your colleagues.

A very important guideline here is that the action verbs you choose must always express what your character is *overtly and explicitly trying to achieve* with a particular thought, not what he or she might be *thinking or plotting under the surface*. This is because all actions are played in order to have a particular effect on another character or characters, so unless the other character is able to experience that effect, the action cannot be said to have been 'played'. An example of this can be found in the first speech of our scene, when Jack enters Algernon's flat.

1. How are you, my dear Ernest? – I WELCOME

Algernon greets Jack enthusiastically, and we know from reading the play that Algernon is glad to see Jack because he is keen to find out who Cecily is. Yet whatever the underlying intention, the action is still I WELCOME. This is because Algernon is fully intending to trick Jack into revealing information, so the last thing he wants to do is put Jack on his guard. For this reason you would not choose a verb such as I LURE or I CAPTURE for this thought, even if this is the *underlying intention. The action verb always expresses what is played on the surface.* The subtext affects the choice of verb, but you should never choose a verb that expresses the subtext and not the text.

Algernon's second thought is certainly a more direct pursuit of his objective, but the verb is merely I QUESTION, not I INTERROGATE or I PROBE, much stronger verbs that would certainly make Jack suspicious.

2

  2. What brings you up to town?' – I QUESTION

However, even though the action verbs must reflect what the character is *doing with the text*, not what he is *thinking in the subtext*, the subtext is still an essential source of information for the actor. If you look at Jack's first speech, for example, the action verbs are less obvious, and it is necessary to 'mine' the subtext in order to make a clear choice of action verb. This speech might best be divided into three thoughts:

  1. Oh, pleasure, pleasure! – I BRUSH OFF
  2. What else should bring one anywhere? – I CONVINCE
  3. Eating as usual, I see, Algy! – I CRITICISE

The first thought is a response to Algernon's question, but here you will need to pause and ask a key question: 'Is Jack speaking the truth?' If it is *true* that Jack has come to London purely for pleasure, you might choose a verb such as 'I AMUSE', 'I INVOLVE' or even 'I EXCITE'. However, we know that Jack has come expressly to propose to Gwendolen, and that this intention is uppermost in his mind, which suggests that he is deliberately misleading Algernon.

It is important at this early stage of Actioning to know whether or not your character is speaking the truth, as this can often make a huge difference to the way you interpret their action. However, I would not use I MIS-LEAD as an action verb, any more than I would use I DECEIVE or I FOOL. The problem with such verbs is that they are defined more by what the actor does *not* do than by what he does. If they are played overtly, they become transparent; if covertly then they disappear as actions. In this case I would use a verb such as I DISMISS or I BRUSH OFF, as Jack implies that the question is irrelevant and needs no serious answer. In other words, by playing an action verb that *hides* rather than *reveals* the subtext, Jack *does* attempt to mislead Algernon, but he does so by playing a strong verb which conceals the act of misleading!

The second thought, therefore, rather than being just a harmless witticism, might be seen as an attempt to convince Algernon of the truth of the first thought. I CONVINCE would be my choice.

The final thought of this speech probably has the intention to divert Algernon's attention away from his enquiry, but here I would not choose 'I DIVERT' as the action verb. The diversion is certainly there, but 'I CRITICISE' would probably be a better verb, because it expresses more accurately what Jack is actually doing, which is to affront Algernon's vanity and put him on the defensive.

Algernon's reply shows us that Jack has succeeded.

> 1. I believe it is customary in good society to take some
>   slight refreshment at five o'clock. – I OUTCLASS

Algernon's first thought on this line is a direct response to Jack's mockery, which he counters by taking a superior tone. I would probably choose the verb I OUTCLASS here. Algernon regards himself as the epitome of urban male sophistication, and he uses his sense of social superiority to crush any criticism. Having done so, he delivers his second thought:

> 2. Where have you been since last Thursday? – I QUIZ

This is clearly a return to his main objective and to his line of enquiry, so the verb could be I QUIZ.

One can assume that Algernon has frequently questioned Jack about his home life, and that Jack is quite accustomed to deflecting such questions, as his reply here indicates:

> 1. In the country. – I SHRUG OFF

Algernon perceives this action, but instead of intensifying the questioning, he attempts to needle Jack into revealing more about his country life by adopting a scornful tone:

> 1. What on earth do you do there? – I DERIDE

Unfortunately for Algernon, the ploy fails, and Jack continues to discourage all interest and enquiry.

> 1. When one is in town one amuses oneself. When one is in the country one amuses other people. – I DISAPPOINT
>
> 2. It is excessively boring. – I DISCOURAGE

Algernon counters by probing Jack's vague and glib statement for detail, which Jack can't provide. He is able to use the stronger verb I PROBE without arousing Jack's suspicions because they are now in conversation:

> 1. And who are the people you amuse? – I PROBE

Jack has no answer to this, but tries to maintain the deception, in this case by trying to make Algernon think that there is nothing of any interest to find out.

1. Oh, neighbours, neighbours. – I BORE

Algernon pursues the issue, artfully mentioning Shropshire as the county Jack claims to live in, in the hope Jack will give himself away and reveal the actual location.

1. Got nice neighbours in your part of Shropshire? – I PURSUE

Jack is not thrown by this, however, and takes the opportunity to WARN Algernon about the perils of the country, presumably in order to dissuade him from showing any further interest.

1. Perfectly horrid! Never speak to one of them! – I WARN

Algernon's reply reveals that he has exposed the holes in Jack's story, perhaps hoping to throw Jack into a state of confusion:

1. How immensely you must amuse them! – I OUTWIT

He then almost casually throws in another question, in the expectation that Jack will be flustered and give himself away:

2. By the way, Shropshire is your county, is it not? – I NUDGE

Jack is now indeed flustered. He has clearly forgotten his earlier claim to live in Shropshire, and for a moment struggles to get his bearings:

1. Eh? Shropshire? – I STALL
2. Yes, of course. – I REASSURE

His hesitation confirms Algernon's suspicions, and in order to prevent further questioning, Jack quickly takes the attention elsewhere:

3. Hallo! – I STARTLE

4. Why all these cups? – I QUIZ

5. Why cucumber sandwiches? – I PRESS

6. Why such reckless extravagance in one so young? –
I TEASE

7. Who is coming to tea? – I INTERROGATE

2

By this time, Algernon has realised that, although Jack is a very poor liar, he will always stop short of revealing the crucial information. However, Jack's interest in Algernon's visitors reminds him that Jack has a soft spot for Gwendolen, and that this weakness can be exploited. Nevertheless he maintains his nonchalant air, not wishing to alert Jack:

1. Oh! merely Aunt Augusta and Gwendolen. – I BRUSH OFF

Safely off the subject of his country home, and delighted that he will get to meet Gwendolen so soon, Jack drops his guard and allows himself a moment of openness:

1. How perfectly delightful! – I INSPIRE

Conscious of the need to get the upper hand, Algernon now seizes the opportunity to remind Jack that there are serious obstacles in his way:

1. Yes, that is all very well; but I'm afraid Aunt Augusta
won't quite approve of your being here. – I WORRY

Disconcerted, Jack demands an explanation:

1. May I ask why? – I INTERROGATE

Having succeeded in worrying Jack, Algernon proceeds to take a moral and disapproving tone about Jack's relationship with Gwendolen, styling himself as Gwendolen's male protector.

1. My dear fellow, the way you flirt with Gwendolen is
perfectly disgraceful. – I ACCUSE

Artfully, however, Algernon then allows Jack to hear that his feelings for Gwendolen are reciprocated, thereby encouraging him to keep pursuing his goal.

> 2. It's almost as bad as the way Gwendolen flirts with you. – I DISGUST

The interesting thing about this last action is that its real intention is the *opposite* of what is actually played. Algernon's real intention here is to HEARTEN Jack, ensuring that he doesn't give up hope of marrying Gwendolen, yet the action he plays seems like an attempt to make Jack think less of her. Such 'fake' actions are typical of deceivers like Algernon. However, the action verb must still be played with as much conviction as if it were sincere – possibly even overplayed. If the actor is thinking the right thought, the irony will not be lost on the audience.

In any case, Jack falls for this ploy and hastens to reassure Algernon that his intentions are entirely honourable:

> 1. I am in love with Gwendolen. – I REASSURE
>
> 2. I have come up to town expressly to propose to her. – I IMPRESS

Jack clearly hopes that the mention of a proposal will make Algernon accept the liaison with Gwendolen and offer his support. Algernon, however, neatly sidesteps this by refusing to take the whole thing seriously:

> 1. I thought you had come up for pleasure? – I DEFLATE
>
> 2. ...I call that business. – I MOCK

Jack is annoyed to have his feelings mocked, and attempts to shame Algernon into a more empathic attitude.

> 1. How utterly unromantic you are! – I SHAME

Algernon counters this by reminding Jack that mar-
riages in their class and era are largely concerned with
ensuring the preservation of wealth and status. This
may be true, but Algernon's intention here is to make
it clear that his support cannot be taken for granted:

1. I really don't see anything romantic in proposing. –
   I AWAKEN

Algernon then draws a clear distinction between love
and marriage, encouraging Jack to remain in his state
of romantic passion rather than seek to make his relationship official. This is one of those moments where
you might, if playing Algernon, have to sit and think
for a moment about precisely why Algernon does this.
To fulfil his main objective, it would surely be better
for him to offer his support in exchange for information about Cecily (which he does openly later in the
scene). In any case, Algernon clearly does not expect
to dissuade Jack from his mission. Moreover, the play
tells us that Algernon will himself be engaged to be
married within a few days, so he is clearly not as
opposed to marriage as he claims.

There are two (or more) possible explanations for
Algernon's attitude, each of which is partly speculative
but still entirely possible:

* It could be that many of Algernon's playboy
  friends have not only recently become engaged
  or got married, but also become nauseatingly
  sentimental in the process. If this is the case,
  then perhaps Algernon takes a short detour
  from his main objective and momentarily plays
  a counter-objective, urging Jack not to go the
  same way.

2

- It could also be that Algernon continues to deride Jack's marital ambitions because he wants to provoke Jack into a state of frustration and absolute determination to pursue his goal, thereby strengthening Algernon's hand.

If the first of these possibilities is chosen, the actions might look like this:

2. It is very romantic to be in love. – I INFLAME

3. But there is nothing romantic about a definite proposal. – I DOUSE

4. Why, one may be accepted. – I WARN

5. One usually is, I believe. – I SCARE

6. Then the excitement is all over. – I DEPRESS

7. The very essence of romance is uncertainty. – I INSPIRE

8. If ever I get married, I'll certainly try to forget the fact. – I SILENCE

With these action choices, Algernon is genuinely sounding off about the way marriage traps young men, and issuing an honest warning. If the action-verb choices are based on the second possibility, however, the actions might look more like this.

2. It is very romantic to be in love. – I SOFTEN

3. But there is nothing romantic about a definite proposal. – I MOCK

4. Why, one may be accepted. One usually is, I believe. – I TEASE

5. Then the excitement is all over. – I UNNERVE

6. The very essence of romance is uncertainty. – I DISCONCERT

7. If ever I get married, I'll certainly try to forget the fact. – I PROVOKE

Here, Algernon is taking a deliberately and overtly mocking attitude towards Jack's aspirations. His intention is not to convince, nor does he try to conceal the insincerity of his argument. In this case he is simply trying to provoke Jack into a state of indignation and recklessness.

These two different interpretations stand as a reminder that choosing action verbs is never an exact science, and there is rarely only one possibility. Fundamentally, you are looking for verbs that reflect and encapsulate *your* understanding of the text, which means that your interpretation will always be the key determinant. When you start to speak the text, therefore, you should be clear about both the verbs themselves, and the character intention that drives them. In some cases, the process of playing those actions in rehearsal will lead you to change your mind about your interpretation and about the verbs, as I shall demonstrate in later chapters; however, for now the most important thing is just to make clear and informed choices.

Noting Down Your Action Choices

If you are Actioning a scene as a precursor to rehearsal and performance, you will need to note down your action verbs on the text itself, partly for ease of reference, and partly so that there is a strong visual connection, from the start, between the textual thought and the action verb. For the purposes of this book, however, I have recorded the actions from this section of text in tabular format.

ACTIONING

TEXT	ACTION VERB
A: How are you, my dear Ernest?	I GREET
A: What brings you up to town?	I QUESTION
J: Oh, pleasure, pleasure!	I BRUSH OFF
J: What else should bring one anywhere?	I CONVINCE
J: Eating as usual, I see, Algy!	I MOCK
A: I believe it is customary in good society to take some slight refreshment at five o'clock.	I OUTCLASS
A: Where have you been since last Thursday?	I QUIZ
J: In the country.	I SHRUG OFF
A: What on earth do you do there?	I DERIDE
J: When one is in town one amuses oneself. When one is in the country one amuses other people.	I DISAPPOINT
J: It is excessively boring.	I DISCOURAGE
A: And who are the people you amuse?	I PROBE
J: Oh, neighbours, neighbours	I BORE
A: Got nice neighbours in your part of Shropshire?	I PURSUE
J: Perfectly horrid! Never speak to one of them.	I WARN
A: How immensely you must amuse them!	I OUTWIT
A: By the way, Shropshire is your county, is it not?	I NUDGE
J: Eh? Shropshire?	I STALL
J: Yes, of course.	I REASSURE
J: Hallo!	I STARTLE
J: Why all these cups?	I QUIZ
J: Why cucumber sandwiches?	I PRESS

J: Why such reckless extravagance in one so young?	I TEASE
J: Who is coming to tea?	I INTERROGATE
A: **Oh! merely Aunt Augusta and Gwendolen.**	I BRUSH OFF
J: How perfectly delightful!	I INSPIRE
A: Yes, that is all very well; but I'm afraid Aunt Augusta won't quite approve of your being here.	I WORRY
J: May I ask why?	I INTERROGATE
A: My dear fellow, the way you flirt with Gwendolen is perfectly disgraceful.	I ACCUSE
A: It is almost as bad as the way Gwendolen flirts with you.	I DISGUST
J: I am in love with Gwendolen.	I REASSURE
J: **I have come up to town expressly to propose to her.**	I IMPRESS
A: I thought you had come up for pleasure?	I DEFLATE
A:…I call that business.	I SHOCK
J: How utterly unromantic you are!	I SHAME
A: I really don't see anything romantic in proposing.	I AWAKEN
A: It is very romantic to be in love.	I SOFTEN
A: But there is nothing romantic about a definite proposal.	I MOCK
A: Why, one may be accepted. One usually is, I believe.	I TEASE
A: Then the excitement is all over.	I STIR
A: The very essence of romance is uncertainty.	I DISCONCERT
A: If ever I get married, I'll certainly try to forget the fact.	I PROVOKE

2

It can be quite useful to see a scene encapsulated by this table of verbs, because it offers a kind of summary of the scene's journey, and indicates how and where the power shifts within the dialogue.

Of course, as an actor working on a role, you will not be in a position to dictate the action verbs of characters other than your own. Depending on the director's way of working, you may discover your scene partner's action verbs during early rehearsal 'table work', or you may never know precisely what they are. In fact, this is of little importance, because either way you will encounter your scene partner's action verbs when they are played in rehearsal. In Chapter Three, I will be looking at what happens when your choices come up against those of another actor.

Choosing action verbs involves two main skills – being able to analyse text in a simple, uncluttered and logical way, avoiding 'psychobabble' and obfuscation; and being able to identify the right verbs to encapsulate your analysis. Most actors initially struggle with both, but you can develop these skills very quickly with practice. Once you have mastered them, you will find that your whole approach to text changes. You will become much more workmanlike in your analysis, seeking to pinpoint rather than complicate, and always trying to distil the complexity of the play world into a moment of clarity and simplicity.

Subtext and Inner Monologue

The process of thinking about the text and selecting your action verbs will also start to reveal your character's subtext – what he *thinks* but does not *say*. This shifting subtextual journey is known as the character's inner monologue.

Like the action verbs, the inner monologue can be recorded on or next to your script, as a useful aide-memoire to help you recall at a later stage why you made a particular choice. It can also be noted down in tabular form, so that you can view the entire through-line of your character's subtext through a scene, as in the tables following.

Again, these are not the only choices you might make, but merely examples. Algernon and Jack's inner monologues might run as follows:

TEXT	ACTION VERB	INNER MONOLOGUE (ALGERNON)
A: How are you, my dear Ernest?	I GREET	*He looks tense – I'll put him at his ease.*
A: What brings you up to town?	I QUESTION	*I mustn't put him on his guard.*
J: Oh, pleasure, pleasure!	I BRUSH OFF	*He's hiding something.*
J: What else should bring one anywhere?	I CONVINCE	*He's such a bad liar.*
J: Eating as usual, I see, Algy!	I MOCK	*He's always finding fault.*
A: I believe it is customary in good society to take some slight refreshment at five o'clock.	I OUTCLASS	*Ha! That told him!*
A: Where have you been since last Thursday?	I QUIZ	*I'll make him feel guilty for abandoning me.*
J: In the country.	I SHRUG OFF	*He's getting all evasive again.*
A: What on earth do you do there?	I DERIDE	*I'll just wind him up a bit.*
J: When one is in town one amuses oneself. When one is in the country one amuses other people.	I DISAPPOINT	*Oh dear, he's not going to rise to it.*
J: It is excessively boring.	I DISCOURAGE	*He really doesn't want to talk about it.*
A: And who are the people you amuse?	I PROBE	*I'll just keep pushing till he gives himself away.*
J: Oh, neighbours, neighbours	I BORE	*He's quite clearly bluffing.*
A: Got nice neighbours in your part of Shropshire?	I PURSUE	*Let's see if he walks into my trap.*
J: Perfectly horrid! Never speak to one of them.	I WARN	*He didn't even notice!*
A: How immensely you must amuse them!	I OUTWIT	*He's not going to let anything out.*
A: By the way, Shropshire is your county, is it not?	I NUDGE	*Let's see how he reacts.*
J: Eh? Shropshire?	I STALL	*I knew it!*
J: Yes, of course.	I REASSURE	*He is such a bad liar!*
J: Hallo!	I STARTLE	*Eh?*
J: Why all these cups?	I QUIZ	*He's trying to change the subject.*

J: Why cucumber sandwiches?	I PRESS	*Ah, he's noticed.*
J: Why such reckless extravagance in one so young?	I TEASE	*He really isn't funny.*
J: Who is coming to tea?	I INTERROGATE	*He's hoping it's Gwendolen!*
A: Oh! merely Aunt Augusta and Gwendolen.	I BRUSH OFF	*Let's see how he reacts to this.*
J: How perfectly delightful!	I ENTHUSE	*Got him!*
A: Yes, that is all very well; but I'm afraid Aunt Augusta won't quite approve of your being here.	I WARN	*I'll make him sweat.*
J: May I ask why?	I INTERROGATE	*He's worried now!*
A: My dear fellow, the way you flirt with Gwendolen is perfectly disgraceful.	I ACCUSE	*I'll make him really panic…*
A: It is almost as bad as the way Gwendolen flirts with you.	I DISGUST	*…and then throw him a lifeline.*
J: I am in love with Gwendolen.	I REASSURE	*He's so naive – he thinks love is enough!*
J: **I have come up to town expressly to propose to her.**	I IMPRESS	*Ha! I knew he was hiding something!*
A: I thought you had come up for pleasure?	I DEFLATE	*Does he expect me to get all sentimental?*
A:…I call that business.	I SHOCK	*This will upset him!*
J: How utterly unromantic you are!	I SHAME	*Got him!*
A: I really don't see anything romantic in proposing.	I AWAKEN	*Let's rub it in a bit…*
A: It is very romantic to be in love.	I SOFTEN	*…cast myself as the true romantic…*
A: But there is nothing romantic about a definite proposal.	I MOCK	*…and make him doubt himself.*
A: Why, one may be accepted. One usually is, I believe.	I TEASE	*Then irritate him with my frivolity…*
A: Then the excitement is all over.	I STIR	*…and my playboy attitudes…*
A: The very essence of romance is uncertainty.	I DISCONCERT	*…make him feel insecure…*
A: If ever I get married, I'll certainly try to forget the fact.	I PROVOKE	*…then give him the moral high ground.*

TEXT	ACTION VERB	INNER MONOLOGUE (JACK)
A: How are you, my dear Ernest?	I GREET	*He's unusually friendly – must be up to something.*
A: What brings you up to town?	I QUESTION	*He mustn't know why I'm here!*
J: Oh, pleasure, pleasure!	I BRUSH OFF	*I'll play him at his own game.*
J: What else should bring one anywhere?	I CONVINCE	*Not sure he believes me.*
J: Eating as usual, I see, Algy!	I MOCK	*I'll just change the subject.*
A: I believe it is customary in good society to take some slight refreshment at five o'clock.	I OUTCLASS	*Good, I've wound him up.*
A: Where have you been since last Thursday?	I QUIZ	*He's asking questions again.*
J: In the country.	I SHRUG OFF	*I need to put him off.*
A: What on earth do you do there?	I DERIDE	*He's probing again!*
J: When one is in town one amuses oneself. When one is in the country one amuses other people.	I DISAPPOINT	*This'll put him off!*
J: It is excessively boring.	I DISCOURAGE	*Ha! He hates bores!*
A: And who are the people you amuse?	I PROBE	*Damn! He won't let it go!*
J: Oh, neighbours, neighbours	I BORE	*I haven't a clue what to say.*
A: Got nice neighbours in your part of Shropshire?	I PURSUE	*Why's he so interested all of a sudden?*
J: Perfectly horrid! Never speak to one of them.	I WARN	*Let's really put him off.*
A: How immensely you must amuse them!	I OUTWIT	*Oh dear, I've contradicted myself. Oh well…*
A: By the way, Shropshire is your county, is it not?	I NUDGE	*What's he saying?*
J: Eh? Shropshire?	I STALL	*He lost me there. Oh no, wait a minute…*
J: Yes, of course.	I REASSURE	*Nearly slipped up there. Hope he didn't notice.*
J: Hallo!	I STARTLE	*Quick, change the subject.*
J: Why all these cups?	I QUIZ	*Could this mean what I think it means?*

J: Why cucumber sandwiches?	I PRESS	*It must be for Lady Bracknell!*
J: Why such reckless extravagance in one so young?	I TEASE	*I'll tease him into telling me.*
J: Who is coming to tea?	I INTERROGATE	*Come on, tell me!*
A: Oh! merely Aunt Augusta and Gwendolen.	I BRUSH OFF	*I knew it!*
J: How perfectly delightful!	I ENTHUSE	*That has made my day!*
A: Yes, that is all very well; but I'm afraid Aunt Augusta won't quite approve of your being here.	I WARN	*What's he talking about?*
J: May I ask why?	I INTERROGATE	*Tell me, for God's sake! I need to know!*
A: My dear fellow, the way you flirt with Gwendolen is perfectly disgraceful.	I ACCUSE	*Oh, is that all? But my intentions are honourable!*
A: It is almost as bad as the way Gwendolen flirts with you.	I DISGUST	*So she does love me!*
J: I am in love with Gwendolen.	I REASSURE	*You can all relax because I have deep feelings.*
J: **I have come up to town expressly to propose to her.**	I IMPRESS	*And what's more, I am a man of honour!*
A: I thought you had come up for pleasure?	I DEFLATE	*Oh no, he's going to get all cynical!*
A:…I call that business.	I SHOCK	*Why on earth is this man my friend?*
J: How utterly unromantic you are!	I SHAME	*He has no poetry in his soul!*
A: I really don't see anything romantic in proposing.	I AWAKEN	*Oh, these Londoners!*
A: It is very romantic to be in love.	I SOFTEN	*Oh, he does believe in love, then.*
A: But there is nothing romantic about a definite proposal.	I MOCK	*It's just marriage he doesn't like.*
A: Why, one may be accepted. One usually is, I believe.	I TEASE	*Does he think I don't want to be accepted?*
A: Then the excitement is all over.	I STIR	*Oh dear, is it?*
A: The very essence of romance is uncertainty.	I DISCONCERT	*Not for me – I hate uncertainty – it makes me anxious.*
A: If ever I get married, I'll certainly try to forget the fact.	I PROVOKE	*Now that's going too far.*

2

The inner monologue is an essential tool for the actor. Like the actions themselves, it should always be written next to the script – in pencil – because it will inevitably change and evolve during rehearsal. Action verbs and inner monologue should always be worked on together, because they have a complementary relationship. The inner monologue tracks the shifting subtextual journey, whereas the action verbs are the series of outward strategies employed by the character to manipulate and affect the other character. In performance, the inner monologue lends the spoken text *resonance* (making us believe that the words are driven from inner feelings and intentions) while the action verbs provide *dynamic* (making us believe that the character is in a relationship with the other character and constantly reacting to them).

Playing the Actions

Once you have made your initial action-verb choices and written them into your text, you will need to go through a series of processes to help you own and embody these actions within the acting space. The rest of this book is devoted to the means by which you can use the action verbs as guides and pointers through the early stages of rehearsal.

Speaking the Actions

As you start to consider the relationship between the words on the page, the action verbs you have chosen and the realisation of those choices through the spoken voice, you should quickly become aware of the scope – or possibly the limitations – of your own vocal range, in terms of pitch, volume, tone, pace and resonance. You may also be surprised at how little of that range you employ in your everyday life. It could be that in real life you rely more on facial expression, gesture, coded language and implied subtext than on clear, specific and contrasting vocal choices.

If we look at the opening thoughts of the *Importance of Being Earnest* scene, it becomes clear just how much work the voice needs to do in order to 'land' the action, even before we start to consider the body. In the table below I have listed a series of vocal possibilities which you might try out in order to play your chosen action verbs. As ever, these are not the 'correct' choices but merely possibilities.

TEXT	ACTION VERB	VOCAL CHOICES
A: How are you, my dear Ernest?	I GREET	Pitch goes up, as does volume, serving the convention of greeting a guest effusively. Vowel sounds elongated, especially on stressed syllables, to place emphasis on the positive feelings aroused by Ernest's arrival.
A: What brings you up to town?	I QUESTION	Pitch and volume down as Algernon adopts a slightly conspiratorial tone.
J: Oh, pleasure, pleasure!	I BRUSH OFF	High pitch, medium volume, slightly drawled vowel sounds and falling inflexions as Jack attempts a casual tone.
J: What else should bring one anywhere?	I CONVINCE	Slightly lower pitch, shortened vowels to conceal any emotional agenda and strong consonants to make the argument convincing.
J: Eating as usual, I see, Algy!	I MOCK	Slightly increased volume and lengthened vowel sounds to support the mockery and divert attention away from Algernon's question.
A: I believe it is customary in good society to take some slight refreshment at five o'clock.	I OUTCLASS	Modulated pitch and volume, shortened vowels and strong consonants, to maintain calm high status.
A: Where have you been since last Thursday?	I QUIZ	Pitch goes up, vowels lengthen into a slightly petulant quality as Algernon disguises a highly calculated question as a laddish 'throwaway'.

Actors in early training, despite having identified their action verbs with clarity and intelligence, often seem to have difficulty actually 'delivering' those verbs through the voice. It is not enough just to *think* the action unless you actually play it! When challenged, some actors express surprise that the action verb is not coming across in the voice. Many seem to have a horror of sounding 'over the top', which makes them pull back from finding their full range and from experimenting with vocal qualities.

3

You may find, therefore, that a certain amount of vocal exploration is required, not just to find the quality of each action, but to experience the shifts from one action to the next. Like a pianist practising scales or an athlete doing stretches, you may have to engage in 'vocal gymnastics', heightening the choices by taking them to the top and bottom of your pitch range, the outer limits of nasal and chest resonance and the lengthening or shortening of the vowel sounds, to name but a few examples. Just the simple act of shifting the pitch of the next action to contrast with the last one can allow you to experience the corresponding thought-change as something visceral and real, as opposed to something head-based and conjectural.

All this may sound a bit like a voice class, but the point here is that you are not *learning* vocal technique, but finding opportunities to *apply* your technique in order to fulfil both the demands of the text and the demands which you have placed upon yourself by choosing a particular verb. By accepting the *permissions* of your own choices you can start to open up the vocal possibilities and use your vocal skills in clear and specific contexts.

Using your full vocal range will also require you to breathe more deeply and use more breath control in order to power your choices. The moment you do this, you will start to 'live' your action choices and to *think* as the character. You will also feel your body becoming more involved in the action as impulses start to happen, and as a result you should find yourself inflecting lines in a spontaneous and nuanced way, rather than just giving yourself technical instructions. You are now ready to start reading the text as a dialogue with your scene partner(s).

Reading the Scene

With the text in front of you, start by doing a readthrough of a scene with your fellow actors, ensuring that each thought is delivered in the manner of the chosen verb by making strong and clear vocal shifts, so that a listener, even if they didn't know the precise verb you had chosen, would at least get a sense of the *quality* of each action and the location of the thought-changes. At this stage you don't have to worry too much about plot, objective, given circumstances or subtext – your main aim is to find a synthesis between the words of the text, the chosen action verb and your corresponding vocal choices.

For the first few readings you also do not need to worry too much about 'through-line' or inner monologue – it is more important that you simply 'land' each action and allow yourself to experience the action choices of the other actors as you hear them. You may have to do this quite a few times, so that you can get used to the particular demands these action-verb choices make on your vocal range, and get the feel of the shifts in energy, pitch and volume. Whatever you do, try not to underplay any action. At this stage you can be larger than life!

It is also important that during these readings you allow your lines and those of your scene partner to find their natural shared rhythm, so that the actions you play are in direct and uncensored response to what you hear from the other actor. It is very important that you do not stop the flow of your breath or allow yourself to make intellectual choices on the text. With the action verbs written clearly and legibly next to the text, you should be able to pick them up and deliver them as part of the text, without falling out of relationship with your fellow actor.

What you will discover is that the script suddenly lifts off the page and is carried along with an extraordinary energy. By the second or third reading you will also find that the vocal shifts you are making between actions start to become part of the conversation you are having with the other actor. In other words, your action verbs, and the vocal choices emerging from those verbs, are now being played as reactions to what you hear, almost without you realising it. This reactive element is something that most actors do naturally as they discover the *flow* of the spoken text. This flow will bring about small but perceptible changes to the rhythm, pace and musicality of your vocal delivery, but should not blur your actions nor fuse them into each other. If you find this happening you will need to return to your choices and embed them even more fully.

3

Learning the Lines with the Actions

The next stage is to learn the lines and the action verbs together, so that each spoken line automatically evokes the idea of its accompanying action verb. This is a very important point within your early rehearsal work. I have worked with actors who dutifully 'action' their texts, yet don't subsequently *learn* the actions with the lines, with the result that, from the point when they come 'off book', the actions, along with much of the analysis they have done on the text, will have simply vanished.

Having learned the lines and the actions together, you need to think of each new thought not as something predetermined, but as a response to the other actor. You know what your next line is (the what), and you know the action verb associated with it (the how), but you don't know what your next line will be a reaction to (the why), until you have seen and experienced what the other actor does in that moment.

Actions as Reactions

Very often, when we are having conversations or arguments in real life, we are constantly watching the other person, gauging how they are responding to us and anticipating what they are going to say. Even when they don't actually speak we still react to them. We might react to their silence, to their non-verbal responses, or to what we assume they are thinking. As an actor your job is to remain faithful to the text and to the action verbs, but at the same time find a *reason*, in the other actor's behaviour, for speaking those particular words, and playing that particular action verb.

These reactive moments will not change the text, nor the action verb, but will *condition* the way in which the line emerges.

'But what if, when I react to another actor, my impulse is to say the line with a different action?' actors often protest. My answer to this is that, all too often, the 'impulsive' response you have to other actors, when you start to rehearse, is not actually the *character's* response within the given circumstances of the play, but rather *your own* reaction within your own given circumstances. In other words, at the point when you start to get the script onto its feet, you have probably not fully entered into the imaginary world of the character and the play, which means that there can be confusion between what your *character* would do in his world and his circumstances, and what *you* would do in yours.

The action verbs you have chosen, and which you are now starting to vocalise, represent your reading and analysis of the text. They are a fusion between your interpretation of the actual words and your understanding, based on the text as a whole, of the given circumstances and character objectives. When you play your chosen verbs in reaction to another actor, however, you discover the third element, which is your precise reason, in that moment, for wanting to play that action. The action itself does not usually need to change – what changes is the moment, which in turn affects the precise way the action is delivered, as you find yourself responding to the other actor.

I would always ask actors, therefore, to stick to their action choices and see how they work if played as *reactions* to other actors. Invariably actors comment (often with amazement), that sticking to the action verbs actually liberates them from habitual reactions, stimulates thought, offers new and interesting permissions, and stops them from getting fixed in a single mode of delivery. This, as we will see later, also has a physical and spatial dimension.

So how does it work? If we take a sample section of our dialogue from *The Importance of Being Earnest*, we can start to investigate this phenomenon and see how and why it does *not* block or stifle the actor's creativity, but instead allows access to the world of the play.

TEXT	ACTION VERB
A: My dear fellow, the way you flirt with Gwendolen is perfectly disgraceful.	I ACCUSE
A: It is almost as bad as the way Gwendolen flirts with you.	I DISGUST
J: I am in love with Gwendolen.	I REASSURE
J: I have come up to town expressly to propose to her.	I IMPRESS
A: I thought you had come up for pleasure?	I DEFLATE
A: ...I call that business.	I SHOCK
J: How utterly unromantic you are!	I SHAME
A: I really don't see anything romantic in proposing.	I COUNTER

Algernon's first action in this section (according to our interpretation) is I DISGUST. Algernon is deliberately expressing distaste for the way Jack has behaved with Gwendolen and inviting Jack to be disgusted at himself. On one level, this distaste is the expression of Algernon's personal reaction to seeing his friend and his cousin flirting, but there is another, more significant aspect to his comment too, which is the *social impropriety*. Algernon is implying that Jack and Gwendolen have overstepped the mark and have incurred the disapproval of Lady Bracknell. In a world where social acceptance is everything, this is potentially extremely damaging to Jack's aspirations.

A twenty-first-century actor playing Jack might easily miss this, responding only (with annoyance) to Algernon's 'younger-brother' attitude to the romance. Left to yourself you might play a different action, such as I CHIDE or I DERIDE, yet here you are *required* to play I REASSURE, followed by I IMPRESS, which are much more vulnerable actions. By sticking to the verbs you have chosen and not going with the first impulse, you can often discover something about the character – in this case, his awareness of the rigidity of the social order (and his vulnerability to it) and, of course, the need to appease Lady Bracknell.

Algernon's reaction is to DEFLATE, and then to SHOCK. We know from our analysis of the scene and the play so far that it is very much in Algernon's interests to make Jack understand that a proposal of marriage is not a natural expression of romantic love, but a business contract governed by money and social position. The need to SHOCK Jack out of his romantic sentimentality arises directly from Algernon's own determination to penetrate Jack's hidden country life, not merely from a desire to make a witty comment. For this reason the action verbs are strong and uncompromising, rather than the lighter I TEASE or I BAIT, which might seem the obvious choices at first glance.

3

Careful choice of action verbs can help you to bridge the gap, from quite an early point in rehearsal, between your own understanding or reading of a situation and that which the character might have in a different time or place. Additionally, the action verbs force you to connect each thought back to the character objective, so that every line of text is powered from a real need, rooted firmly in the given circumstances, even if the dialogue appears at first glance to be quite light and frothy. A classic example of this occurs in Shakespeare's *As You Like It*, where Rosalind, disguised as a young man, engages in apparently light-hearted role-play games with Orlando. The dialogue initially seems very playful and whimsical, yet unless both characters play strong action verbs reflecting the strength of their very real passions and desires, the audience quickly loses interest and the games lose their danger and significance.

Action verbs can bridge other gaps, too. It is all too easy to judge a character, or the main contention of a scene, to be trivial and unimportant, and to play it as such. Your job as an actor, however, is to find the truth of a scene by connecting to and understanding the character's objective, no matter how trivial it may appear at first glance. A scene about some minor domestic issue can be highly significant to the characters themselves, even if that significance is not immediately apparent from the script. Action verbs can help you uncover the underlying power struggle in any scene, provided you choose strong verbs and commit to them!

It is important for you to understand that action verbs do not block your capacity to respond in the moment, nor do they force you into a fixed response. Action verbs merely limit the range of your possible responses to within the scope of a particular verb. Within those limits many variables are open to you – in the moment of reaction you can vary pitch, tone, volume and a host of other things, not randomly, but according to:

3

a. What the other actor actually does and says, and…

b. …what you perceive he *might* do or say.

If we revisit the same excerpt from *The Importance of Being Earnest* we can see that each thought/action change relies on the stimulus provided by the other character. The suggestions below are once again just illustrative possibilities of what those stimuli might be:

TEXT	ACTION VERB	REACTS TO:
A: My dear fellow, the way you flirt with Gwendolen is perfectly disgraceful.	I ACCUSE	Jack's slightly affronted air. Algernon needs to make Jack see that he is the wrongdoer, not the wronged.
A: It is almost as bad as the way Gwendolen flirts with you.	I DISGUST	Jack's incredulity at being thus accused.
J: I am in love with Gwendolen.	I REASSURE	The implied sordidness or impropriety of his relationship with Gwendolen.
J: I have come up to town expressly to propose to her.	I IMPRESS	Algernon's sardonic reaction to the notion of 'being in love'.

A: I thought you had come up for pleasure?	I DEFLATE	Jack's pomposity.
A: ...I call that business.	I SHOCK	Jack's puzzlement.
J: How utterly unromantic you are!	I SHAME	Algernon's failure to be moved in any way.
A: I really don't see anything romantic in proposing.	I COUNTER	Jack's disapproval.
A: It is very romantic to be in love.	I COUNTER	The possibility that Jack is confusing love with marriage.
A: But there is nothing romantic in a definite proposal.	I MOCK	The fact that Jack is about to interrupt.

In this respect, action verbs are the actor's best friend. Faced with too many possibilities and no clear track to follow, many actors fall into one or more of the following:

- Ceasing to listen to the other actor and speaking the lines in a fixed way.

- Becoming passive and low-energy through failing to energise from the other actor.

- Putting 'bids' on the lines by trying to inject energy to new thoughts, but not through listening or responding to the other actor.

The process of Actioning the text, as we have seen, is a 'dialogue' between the actor and the text. 'I will make these choices,' you say, 'because this is what I perceive the text to be telling me. I think I know *what* the action verbs are, and I have some ideas, from the given circumstances and scene objective, about *why* the character might play those actions. What I don't know is the *precise* reason, in the moment, that I choose to play that action, and therefore precisely *how*, in the moment, it will manifest itself. For this reason I am dependent on the other actor and on the moment, to reveal these things to me.'

If we think of actions in this way, then the action choices become very like the lines themselves – fixed in one sense and yet infinitely variable in another. Most actors do not kick against the text, because the text offers a richness of crafted language and a wealth of possibilities. It also offers structure, direction and form, which enable you to relax and get on with the business of living each moment. So it is with action verbs – the main difference being that *you* have chosen them and therefore have ownership of them before you even start.

Where actors go wrong with Actioning is in creating fixed 'line-readings' from the action verbs and then assuming that those line-readings are exactly what must be delivered on each line, regardless of what happens in the space or what the other actor does. This misunderstanding of how Actioning works, lies, I believe, at the root of all the reservations that actors express about the technique.

Used correctly, action verbs do not restrict – they confer permissions. Many actors get very anxious about the 'truthfulness' of their impulses. Sometimes that anxiety is so acute that they end up doing nothing at all! Action verbs can take all that anxiety away. If you know you have to play a particular action, especially

3

if it is a strong action, then you also know you need to energise in order to deliver it. To energise you have to breathe, and in the process of taking that breath you come out of your head and into the moment.

Action verbs can also help remove your inhibitions. Just as the text may allow you to say things you would never dare to say in an improvisation, so a strong action, such as I ANNIHILATE or I SEDUCE, can offer you the permissions that come from following an instruction – albeit an instruction that you gave yourself when you analysed the text! By rising vocally and physically to the demand of the action verb, you may find a greater confidence in the rehearsal space.

The process of reading the text in the manner of the chosen action verbs, while simultaneously responding, within the given circumstances, to whatever the other actor is doing and saying, helps you, the actor, gain a deeper understanding of *form*. Too often among young actors there is an unhelpful 'binary' set up between personal impulse on the one hand, and the demands of the production, as articulated by playwright and director, on the other. To put it another way: you assume that to follow the instructions of the director is some kind of artistic surrender to a greater will than your own, and that this surrender will necessarily mean the suppression of your own creative freedom. You do surrender (because you have to), but you do so with reluctance and resentment, concluding that your performance (and the production) would have been so much better had you only been allowed to do what you wanted!

Notwithstanding the fact that there may be some directors who might crush actors' creativity, there is a need for all actors to experience the boundaries of both the text and the action verbs, because it is usually within a fairly narrow range of choices that you become most acutely aware of your impulses. The action verbs not only mediate between your habitual impulses and the demands of the play, but also, by making you aware of the clash between the two, they create a different kind of motive energy. This is the same kind of energy you tap in to in real life when you know that what you would *like* to do or say is entirely inappropriate to the moment and will have significant consequences later. It is the kind of energy that allows you to stay calm when you feel like losing your temper, to be enthusiastic when you feel like giving up, or to fight when you would rather run away. It is a powerful force within you because it is the imposition of your *will* upon your *instinct*, and therefore needs to be strong enough to reverse the direction and nature of your emotional energy.

Many actors struggle with the whole idea of being truly reactive to other actors. They trust neither themselves nor their fellow actors to deliver the 'right' reaction and keep the play on track. Actors therefore often 'fake' reactions, trying (usually unsuccessfully) to convince their audiences that they are reacting to someone else when, in fact, they are 'self-triggering' – working from an inner instruction rather than an outer impulse. This fear of the genuine reactive moment is very real, but that fear can be neutralised if you are working fully within the form of the production. The form becomes the boundary, and within that boundary you will be free to play and respond without fear.

The Physical Dimension of Acting

Up until now we have focused exclusively on Action-ing as an analytical tool and vocal technique, and, for many actors and directors, this is as far as it goes. The idea is that by choosing an action verb you will be motivated to make strong vocal shifts, which in turn requires you to breathe, thereby stimulating impulses and physical/gestural responses. Up to a point this works, particularly in relatively static contexts.

Once you start to play your actions in the space, how-ever, you may notice that both you and your fellow actors seem to want to move physically closer and closer to the 'target' of the action verbs, regardless of the nature of the verbs themselves. This leads to a problem that we call 'pushing into forward space'. Because all action verbs by definition have a psycho-logical *direction of travel* from you to the other actor, the body seems to develop a compulsion to move in that same direction. However, there is just so far that you can travel towards another actor (and they towards you) before you get 'stuck' in forward space, crowding and eyeballing your fellow actor, and with absolutely nowhere left to go. At this point you may still be playing the action verb through the voice, but the body is not involved, other than to carry you for-ward until no more forward motion is possible. In other words, your body, which should be the carrier and amplifier of each specific thought/action, pushes into a place of stasis from where it ceases to signal or indeed communicate anything beyond a vague and generalised forward energy.

So why does this happen? One reason may be that, in a modern urban society, your bodies are probably not used to expressing thought in this way. Even leaving aside the fact that many of our everyday conversations now take place through electronic media, most of us are squeezed into tiny apartments and small crowded spaces, which means that we rarely use our bodies as amplifiers of thought, word and intention, relying instead on the coding of the words themselves and on facial expressions to communicate with others. The theatre actor, on the other hand, needs to be able to use both the spatial 'floor plan' of moves, and a heightened and distilled gestural body language, in order to communicate meaning over significant distances.

To do this requires you to override your habitual physical reticence and train your body to move and carry meaning in a clear, uncluttered and powerful way. The difficulty this presents is one both of permission and impulse – permission because you may fear the impact such large and resounding gestures will make; impulse because your body can only make such moves truthfully when powered by clear intentions. A director can give you permission by blocking a scene to the last detail, but only clarity of intention can make those moves truthful and allow you to own them.

As with so much in the Actioning technique, the solution to this problem lies in the clues provided by the verbs themselves. Many action verbs suggest not just physical gestures, but also spatial and gestural choices

4

in relation to other actors and to objects within the space. These suggestions are sometimes intrinsic to the particular verb (I APPROACH, I DISDAIN, I RETREAT FROM, I ATTACK) but are more often dictated by the context and circumstances in which the verb is played.

If we look again at the second sample dialogue in Chapter One, it is easy to see that each of these verbs – mostly not in isolation, but within a clear knowledge of the context and given circumstances – can suggest a *physical move and gesture* in the space. Very often this move is a change in the spatial relationship between your character and another, or between your character and a particular object. Some verbs might suggest a move *towards*, and some a move *away from* the other character, while others suggest moves in relation to objects within the space. The verbs can also stimulate *gestures* which connect to the move in space and which are also an expression of character intention.

Identifying the physical/spatial dimension of an action verb requires you to enter into yet another dialogue with the text. Using your working knowledge of the character, the relationships and the given circumstances, plus a strong element of spatial imagination, it is possible for you to make choices about how each verb might be physically expressed within the context of that moment. Once again, this is not an exact science; rather it is a way of stopping yourself from becoming 'stuck in your own head', which means that you play the action verbs through your voice while unable to connect those intentions through your body into clear physical and gestural moves.

The physical choices you make will always (like the action verbs themselves) be just *one set of possibilities* for interpreting the text. Even as you read the choices I have made on the sample dialogue, you may well be taking issue with these and making different choices for yourself, and that is as it should be. The point here is not whether you agree with *my* choices, but whether you understand how the action verbs can help *you* discover the physical journey of a scene.

4

The choice of moves and gestures must always be made as part of a 'narrative' of actions and reactions, so that it is never the action verb alone that dictates your choices. You will also need to take into account, as you did when choosing the verbs, the environment, the given circumstances and the subtext. The diagram below illustrates all the different factors that need to be taken into account for each choice. The action verb itself is the *key* determinant but not the *only* determinant. In other words, the physical move can never contradict the action verb, but the other factors may have a strong influence on *how* the action verb is physically expressed.

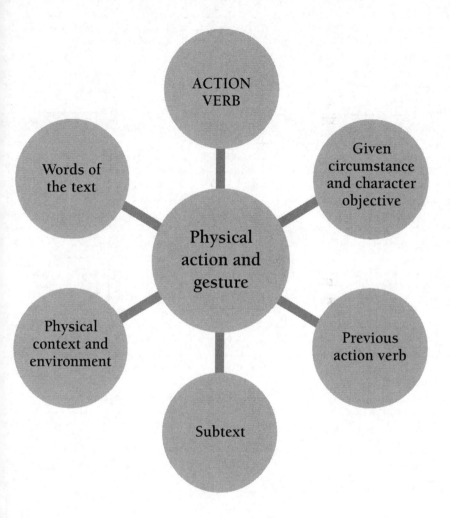

In this sample dialogue, we can construct a table of action verbs and suggested physical moves/gestures on each thought, as follows:

TEXT	ACTION VERB	PHYSICAL POSSIBLITY
F: Morning!	I TEASE	Comes in but does not hug or touch Sam. Surveys him and the room.
S: Hi.	I FREEZE	Backs away.
F: This place is a tip.	I CHASTISE	Circles the mess.
F: You should clear it up.	I GALVANISE	Stops and looks directly at Sam.
S: Why don't *you*?	I SILENCE	Turns away and resumes searching.
F: It's not my flat.	I REMIND	Steps back away from the mess.
F: Looking for something?	I QUESTION	Comes round to get a better view.
S: Nothing important.	I BLOCK	Stops looking, sits down.
F: If it wasn't so messy you wouldn't lose things.	I CRITICISE	Sits down next to him.
S: Yeah thanks for that.	I REBUKE	Turns away from her.
F: What you lost?	I PROBE	Kneels in front of him.
S: Nothing.	I EVADE	Stands up, moves away.
F: Must be something.	I CONFRONT	Stands, confronts him.
S: Just some money.	I PLACATE	Puts hands on her shoulders and starts looking for the money again.
F: Money?	I PRESS	Takes a step towards him.
F: How much money?	I INTERROGATE	Moves round into his eyeline.
S: Just some money, okay?	I DISMISS	Waves her question away, turns away.
F: What money?	I SHAKE	Approaches him. Touches him.
S: It's a loan.	I SATISFY	Turns to her, opens his body.
F: A loan?	I QUERY	Pulls back.
F: Who from?	I QUIZ	Keeps her distance. Folds arms.
S: Rosie.	I SUBMIT TO	Holds up hands, backs off slightly.

The first action verb is I TEASE. I chose this verb because I assumed that Fran would most likely have some kind of response to the fact that Sam has clearly been drunk the night before and is rather dishevelled. This verb (in context) suggests that Fran does not approach Sam directly but teases from a distance, having seen that both he and the flat are not at their best. The text does not tell us that she approaches Sam or kisses him, so we can safely assume that she doesn't. The physical action suggested here is one of surveying the mess from a distance.

Sam's first action, I FREEZE, also implies distance – Sam's objective is to find the lost money, which means that Fran's arrival at this point is highly unwelcome, especially as he knows she is inquisitive and bossy. Under normal circumstances he might have been more polite, but in this context he is hung-over and anxious, and absolutely doesn't want her there.

I CHASTISE might seem to indicate a direct approach, but since Fran is talking about the mess in the room one can assume that she will want to stay in visual contact with the mess while chastising Sam, which again implies distance, but also possibly implies motion, as she takes in each aspect of the room, circling and avoiding the mess around the sofa rather than sitting down. I GALVANISE, on the other hand, is a much more motivational verb, which probably means that Fran stops and looks directly at him. At this stage she probably doesn't go towards him, because she wants him to look at the mess rather than at her.

Sam's next action, I SILENCE, may seem very dominant, but the stage direction '*He resumes searching*' suggests that, far from this being a forward action, he turns away from her. Similarly, Fran's action I REMIND, in this context, could also have a backward direction as she dissociates herself from the mess. I QUESTION, on the other hand, is her response to suddenly noticing a) that Sam is not looking at her, and b) that he is searching for something. In this context, I QUESTION implies a forward action, not to get in his face, but to see what he is doing. Sam BLOCKS her by stopping searching and sitting down.

She CRITICISES him, sitting next to him and seeking physical proximity so that the criticism can be seen as friendly rather than hostile. Within his anxiety, however, Sam is not in the mood for criticism, and he REBUKES her, turning away and refusing to engage. Returning to the lost item, she PROBES, aware of his agitation and wanting him to share the problem with her. She may touch his shoulder, or even shift from the sofa onto the floor so she can get back into his eyeline. Whatever she does, it prompts him to EVADE her, standing up and creating a distance between them so she can't use physical contact to weaken him. This evasion makes her stand up too and CONFRONT him, and the confrontation forces Sam to engage with her, even though he is not ready to reveal all at this point, and he places his hands on her shoulders reassuringly, quickly moving off to resume the search and forestall further questioning.

Fran PRESSES him, taking a step towards him, then realises she needs eye contact and moves round into his eyeline to INTERROGATE. Continuing with the search Sam DISMISSES her with a wave of his arm, upon which she approaches him to SHAKE him, possibly even literally. This stops him, and he decides to open up further with I SATISFY, turning to her and opening his body. On I QUERY she pulls back to observe him, looking for signs of shiftiness and guilt, and seeing what she is looking for, folds her arms to show him she is serious, and QUIZZES him. Finally he SUBMITS TO her, backing off slightly and acknowledging his misdemeanour through his open and submissive body language.

The important issue here is not whether you necessarily agree with these choices (which are, of course, only possibilities or starting positions), but whether it is clear to you within this analysis that action verbs can be more than ways of speaking lines. They can start to 'direct' you as an actor towards choices you might make within the space. Every action can be played in a number of ways, both vocally and physically, and the choices you make will depend on the precise context of the scene. Once you let the action verb suggest physical choices, you will start to experience the space and the other actor differently, as you become more aware of your body, the other actor's body and the space, as significant factors within the dramatic conflict. If one of your choices doesn't work, this will usually be because in making the *wrong* physical move you have awakened your body to a sense of the *right* one, and will thence be in a position to make a different yet equally clear choice.

The choices you make will derive from your understanding of the space, the relationships and the given circumstances, but also from the need to invest each thought with a new and different energy. Sometimes a thought-change may be conveyed only through the

4

voice, but more often it is signalled by a change in physical direction or gesture. Two consecutive but different actions played through the same physical move will feel, both to actors and audience, like the same action played twice. To differentiate between these actions it is necessary to investigate the difference between the verbs, their subtext and their implied intentions, and then to contrast them physically in the space. In the moment of changing direction or making a physical shift into the new action, you will also (provided your breath and torso are released) experience the thought-change as a physical event, which in turn allows you to become more fully immersed in the character and the world of the play.

Taking the action verbs into the space, and exploring the possibilities of playing them in context, allows you to 'stage' the chosen action verbs by asking yourself whether, in a particular context, a verb suggests increasing, decreasing or maintaining the spatial distance between your character and another character. You might also ask whether the verb implies sitting down or standing up, whether there is any physical contact, and whether your character changes position in relation to third characters or objects in the space. All this can be determined, if not as an infallible formula, then as a series of informed choices which stop you getting trapped in forward space and allow thought to be released into moves and gestures, thereby liberating the breath and preventing intentional energy from turning into tension.

Having established your initial physical choices within a scene, your next job is to inhabit those choices. A good way to start is by learning the lines and the actions together, so that you are no longer 'groping' for the action verb with each line. There are many ways to 'peg' the text and the action verb together in your own mind. Some actors do this merely by speaking each thought aloud several times followed by its action verb; others prefer to physicalise the action while speaking the line.

You should then spend some time creating a firm association, in your own mind, between the action verbs and the physical moves in the space. The best way of achieving this is to do an exercise in which you and your scene partner each speak aloud your own action verbs as a kind of dialogue, temporarily replacing the text itself, while you perform the physical moves in the manner of the spoken action. It is best to go through this fairly mechanically a few times in the first instance, simply in order to link the verb and the physical move in your mind and body, but once this has been achieved, you can then start to become properly reactive, so that even while merely speaking the action verb and not the text, you can start to find the motivation for the next action verb from the other actor.

4

ACTION VERB	PHYSICAL POSSIBLITY	REACTIVE MOMENT
I TEASE (FRAN)	Comes in but does not hug or touch Sam. Surveys him and the room.	Reacts to Sam's wild and dishevelled appearance.
I FREEZE (SAM)	Backs away.	Reacts to her mockery, which grates with his own mood.
I CHASTISE (FRAN)	Circles the mess.	Reacts to his coldness and uses the mess to punish him.
I GALVANISE (FRAN)	Stops and looks directly at Sam.	Reacts to the fact that he is ignoring her and speaks to him more directly.
I SILENCE (SAM)	Turns away and resumes searching.	Reacts to her attempt to dominate.
I REMIND (FRAN)	Steps back away from the mess.	Reacts to his suggestion that she should tidy the flat for him.
I QUESTION (FRAN)	Comes round to get a better view.	Reacts to the realisation that his attention is on his search and not on her.
I BLOCK (SAM)	Stops looking, sits down.	Reacts to the fact that she has noticed that he is looking for something.
I CRITICISE (FRAN)	Sits down next to him.	Reacts to the fact that he has sat down.
I REBUKE (SAM)	Turns away from her.	Reacts to her criticism.
I PROBE (FRAN)	Kneels in front of him.	Reacts to him taking offence.
I EVADE (SAM)	Stands up, moves away.	Reacts to her attempt to make him look at her.
I CONFRONT (FRAN)	Stands, confronts him.	Reacts to his evasion and forces him to look at her.
I PLACATE (SAM)	Puts hands on her shoulders and starts looking for the money again.	Reacts to her insistence and tries another approach.
I PRESS (FRAN)	Takes a step towards him.	Reacts to the fact that he has given her only limited information.
I INTERROGATE (FRAN)	Moves round into his eyeline.	Reacts to the fact that he is now busy searching again and not looking at her.
I DISMISS (SAM)	Waves her question away, turns away.	Reacts to her continued questioning.
I SHAKE (FRAN)	Approaches him. Touches him.	Reacts to the fact that he is still not giving her an answer.
I SATISFY (SAM)	Turns to her, opens his body.	Reacts to her touch and decides to accept rather than reject her.
I QUERY (FRAN)	Pulls back.	Reacts to the fact that his body is open but the information is still incomplete.
I QUIZ (FRAN)	Keeps her distance. Folds arms.	Reacts to the fact that, at a distance, she can see an element of shiftiness in him.
I SUBMIT TO (SAM)	Holds up hands, backs off slightly.	Reacts to her suspicion, decides to tell the truth and anticipates her reaction.

By the time you and your scene partner have worked out this series of reactive moments, the action verbs will have ceased to be merely suggestions for inflecting a line of text, and will have become distillations of *moments* in the scene, from which you will be able to create the 'floor plan' of moves and discover the shifting inner journey for both characters. In other words, through the action verbs and the thought processes that they stimulate, you will have discovered, in basic form, the story of the scene. By 'story' I mean the connective logic that links each textual thought with its physical and vocal manifestation to produce a moment, and then stitches these moments together to create a coherent narrative.

This may sound a little inorganic, but like most technical processes, such as piano scales or dance exercises, it is there to provide a set of well-practised possibilities through which, at a later stage of rehearsal or performance, you can channel your impulses. If you think about it, very few of the psychophysical reactions you have in your everyday life are actually new – most are simply versions of habitual reactions which are drawn from your personal gestural 'vocabulary'. Often this vocabulary is quite limited – adequate for everyday life but less so for heightened situations. It is possible that sometimes you find yourself in situations, in real life, for which you have no appropriate physical or vocal response, so that even though your emotions are looking for an outlet, the permission simply isn't there, and the emotions become trapped in an inarticulate and habitual body.

What needs to be absolutely clear at this point is that, when you practise the Actioning technique, you are not looking for a static and unchangeable 'blocking' of a scene, but merely plotting a vocal and physical journey that encapsulates one possible way to tell the story of the scene. From the clarity of that journey you may make many discoveries, but if you start with something clear you will be able to determine whether a new discovery or spontaneous choice *adds clarity* and complexity to the story you are trying to tell, or whether it *blurs* the story and disrupts the inner logic of the scene.

4

Discovering the Physical Form

In the next example, from Act Three of Chekhov's *The Seagull*, we see all of these factors at work in a much more complex dialogue, which also contains a further element: the specific physical activity of one character changing the other's bandage. In this scene the young failed playwright Konstantin (Kostya) is wildly jealous of the writer Trigorin. Trigorin is not only having an affair with Kostya's actress mother Arkadina, but is also about to seduce Nina, the girl Kostya loves. Kostya has attempted to shoot himself, but has only succeeded in inflicting a slight head injury. In this scene he is using the fact of the head wound to solicit sympathy and attention from his mother, who usually either ignores or mocks him.

In this scene the character objectives are clear. Kostya *wants Arkadina to put him first and agree to get rid of Trigorin*. Arkadina, on the other hand, *wants to avoid being blackmailed into making this choice*. Kostya's obstacle is that Arkadina is deeply anxious about growing old and losing her glamour. Kostya, of course, makes her feel old by being her son, while Trigorin makes her feel young by being her lover. Arkadina's obstacle is that Kostya makes her feel guilty for neglecting him and she is scared he will try to kill himself again.

5

KOSTYA. Mother, will you change my bandage, please? / You do it so well.

ARKADINA (*takes some iodine and a box of bandages out of the medicine cabinet*). The doctor's late.

KOSTYA. He said he'd be here by ten, and it's already noon.

ARKADINA. Sit down. / (*Removes his bandage.*) You look as if you're wearing a turban. / Someone came into the kitchen yesterday and asked what nationality you were. / It's almost completely healed. Hardly anything left. (*She kisses him on the forehead.*) / You won't fiddle around with guns again, will you, when I'm not here?

KOSTYA. No, Mother. It was a moment of despair, sheer madness – I just couldn't control myself. / It won't happen again. / (*Kisses her hand*). You have magic hands. / I remember, a long time ago, when you were still acting in the State theatres – I was quite small then – and there was a fight in our yard, and one of the tenants, a washerwoman, got badly beaten. / D'you remember? She was unconscious when they picked her up… you kept going to see her, taking medicines to her, washing her children in the tub. / You don't remember?

ARKADINA. No. (*Applies a fresh bandage.*)

KOSTYA. There were two girls, ballet dancers, living in the same block. They used to drop in for coffee.

ARKADINA. Yes, that I do remember.

KOSTYA. They were very religious.

A pause.

You know, these past few days, I've loved you just as tenderly and as devotedly as when I was a child. / There's no one left for me now, except you. / But why, tell me why has this man come between us?

ARKADINA. You don't understand him, Kostya. / He's a very noble character.

KOSTYA. Yes, and when he heard I was about to challenge him to a duel, his nobility didn't stop him taking the coward's way out. / He's leaving. Saving his skin!

ARKADINA. Oh, what rubbish! / I'm taking him away myself. / Kostya, you may not like our relationship, but you're an intelligent boy, and I have the right to demand that you respect my freedom.

KOSTYA. I respect your freedom, yes, but you must allow me *my* freedom to treat this man how I please. / Noble character, huh! / Look at us, we're practically falling out over him, and he's sitting right now in the drawing room or the garden somewhere, laughing at the pair of us… / working on Nina, trying to convince her he's a genius!

ARKADINA. You take a delight in being nasty to me. / I respect that man, and I'll ask you not to speak ill of him in my presence.

KOSTYA. Well, I don't respect him. / You want me to think he's a genius too, but I'm sorry, I can't lie, / his writing just makes me sick.

ARKADINA. That's pure envy. / People with no talent, but plenty of pretension – that's all they can do, run down genuine talent. / Well, that's scant consolation, I'd say.

KOSTYA (*sarcastically*). Genuine talent! / (*Fiercely.*) If it comes to that, I've got more talent than the whole lot of you! / (*Tears the bandage from his head.*) You people with your stale conventions, you've got the art world in your pocket, you think what you do is the only legitimate, real work, everything else you try to stifle and suppress. / Well, I don't acknowledge you! I don't acknowledge either you or him!

ARKADINA. Decadent!...

KOSTYA. Go back to your cosy little theatre and act in your pathetic, rubbishy plays!

ARKADINA. I've never acted in rubbish. Leave me alone! / You couldn't even write a third-rate farce. / Provincial philistine! / Sponger!

KOSTYA. Miser!

ARKADINA. Tramp!

KOSTYA *sits down and begins quietly weeping.*

Nonentity! / (*Paces up and down in agitation.*) Look, don't cry. There's no need for that. / (*Begins to weep also.*) Don't, please. / (*Kisses his forehead, his cheeks.*) Oh, my darling boy, forgive me. / Forgive your sinful mother. Forgive me, I'm so unhappy.

KOSTYA (*embraces her*). Oh, if only you knew! I've lost everything. / She doesn't love me, I can't write any more. / I've nothing left to live for.

ARKADINA. Don't give up hope. It'll all turn out right. / I'm taking him away now, she'll come to love you again. / (*Wipes away his tears.*) Don't cry. We're friends again, right?

KOSTYA (*kisses her hands*). Yes, Mother.

ARKADINA (*tenderly*). Kostya, make it up with him, too. / We don't want any duels, do we.

KOSTYA. All right. Only please don't make me face him. That's too hard. / I haven't the strength…

As ever, the action-verb choices below are just possibilities, and might not be the same as yours, but for now we can use them to investigate the changing psychophysical relationship between the characters.

5

TEXT	ACTION VERB
K: Mother, will you change my bandage, please?	I CAJOLE
K: You do it so well.	I COMPLIMENT
A: The doctor's late.	I PUNISH
K: He said he'd be here by ten, and it's already noon.	I ENLIST
A: Sit down.	I COMMAND
A: You look as if you're wearing a turban.	I MOCK
A: Someone came into the kitchen yesterday and asked what nationality you were.	I RIDICULE
A: It's almost completely healed. Hardly anything left.	I BELITTLE
A: You won't fiddle around with guns again, will you, when I'm not here?	I INFANTILISE
K: No, Mother.	I OBEY
K: It was a moment of despair, sheer madness – I just couldn't control myself.	I SADDEN
K: It won't happen again	I REASSURE
K: You have magic hands.	I WORSHIP
K: I remember a long time ago, when you were still acting in the State theatres – I was quite small then – and there was a fight in our yard, and one of the tenants, a washerwoman, got badly beaten.	I REMIND
K: She was unconscious when they picked her up… you kept going to see her, taking medicines to her, washing her children in the tub.	I ADMIRE
K: You don't remember?	I NUDGE
A: No.	I EVADE

5

K: There were two girls, ballet dancers, living in the same block. They used to drop in for coffee.	I PROD
A: Yes, that I do remember.	I MEET
K: They were very religious.	I AMUSE
K: You know, these past few days, I've loved you just as tenderly and as devotedly as when I was a child.	I ADORE
K: There's no one left for me now, except you.	I CLING TO
K: But why, tell me why has this man come between us?	I REPROACH
A: You don't understand him, Kostya.	I REBUKE
A: He's a very noble character.	I INSPIRE
K: Yes, and when he heard I was about to challenge him to a duel, his nobility didn't stop him taking the coward's way out.	I CHALLENGE
K: He's leaving. Saving his skin!	I MOCK
A: Oh, what rubbish!	I DERIDE
A: I'm taking him away myself.	I CORRECT
A: Kostya, you may not like our relationship, but you're an intelligent boy, and I have the right to demand that you respect my freedom.	I DISCIPLINE
K: I respect your freedom, yes, but you must allow me *my* freedom to treat this man how I please.	I DEFY
K: Noble character, huh!	I RIDICULE
K: Look at us, we're practically falling out over him, and he's sitting right now in the drawing room or the garden somewhere, laughing at the pair of us...	I AWAKEN
K: working on Nina, trying to convince her he's a genius.	I NEEDLE

A: You take a delight in being nasty to me.	I EXPOSE
A: I respect that man, and I'll ask you not to speak ill of him in my presence.	I SILENCE
K: Well, I don't respect him.	I DEFY
K: You want me to think he's a genius, as you do, but I'm sorry, I can't lie,	I UNDERMINE
K: his writing just makes me sick.	I STAB
A: That's pure envy.	I REBUFF
A: People with no talent, but plenty of pretension – that's all they can do, run down genuine talent.	I SCOLD
A: Well, that's scant consolation, I'd say.	I MOCK
K: Genuine talent!	I RIDICULE
K: If it comes to that, I've got more talent than the whole lot of you!	I BAIT
K: You people with your stale conventions, you've got the art world in your pocket, you think what you do is the only legitimate real work, everything else you try to stifle and suppress!	I DESPISE
K: Well, I don't acknowledge you! I don't acknowledge either you or him!	I REJECT
A: Decadent!...	I SHAME
K: Go back to your cosy little theatre and act in your pathetic, rubbishy plays!	I PROVOKE
A: I've never acted in rubbish. Leave me alone!	I ATTACK
A: You couldn't even write a third-rate farce.	I INSULT
A: Provincial philistine! Sponger!	I PURSUE
K: Miser!	I ACCUSE
A: Tramp! Nonentity!	I SLAP

5

A: Look, don't cry. There's no need for that.	I SUPPRESS
A: Don't, please.	I PLEAD WITH
A: Oh, my darling boy, forgive me, please. Forgive your sinful mother.	I BEG
A: Forgive me, I'm so unhappy.	I ENLIST
K: Oh, if only you knew!	I EMBRACE
K: I've lost everything. She doesn't love me, I can't write any more.	I MOVE
K: I've nothing left to live for.	I ALARM
A: Don't give up hope. It'll all turn out right.	I ENCOURAGE
A: I'm taking him away now, she'll come to love you again.	I REASSURE
A: Don't cry.	I IMPLORE
A: We're friends again, right?	I STEADY
K: Yes, Mother.	I ACCEPT
A: Kostya, make it up with him, too.	I COAX
A: We don't want any duels, do we.	I WARN
K: All right.	I OBEY
K: Only please don't make me face him. That's too hard.	I ENTREAT
K: I haven't the strength…	I WORRY

Now, once again, you can start to link the action verbs to physical moves and gestures within the given circumstances of the scene. As before, this is not supposed to be a definitive or prescriptive way of playing the scene but merely an analysis that you can use to create a particular vocal, physical and spatial 'story', which then becomes the starting point for the creative journey.

Kostya's first action, I CAJOLE, could be played in a number of ways, but one can safely assume that he approaches his mother, possibly even taking her hand, in order to force her into a maternal role. Kostya knows that the ageing Arkadina is reluctant even to acknowledge him as her son, let alone perform acts of maternal solicitude, so by becoming childlike and helpless he is prompting her to relive an earlier stage in their relationship, at a time when she still felt young and glamorous.

Kostya's additional action, I COMPLIMENT, is presumably intended to overcome any hesitation she may express. The physical action here might be to hug her or kiss her hand, which both increases the emotional pressure and physically entraps her.

Arkadina doesn't feel she can openly reject him, but by expressing annoyance at the doctor's lateness, she is PUNISHING Kostya by making it clear that she doesn't feel changing his bandage is her job. She fetches the first-aid box (which allows her to detach herself from him) but expresses impatience in the manner in which she sorts out the bandage.

Kostya, however, rather than rising to this provocation and getting annoyed, merely uses the fact of the doctor's failure to appear, as yet another reason for needing her support, hence I ENLIST. His physical action is probably to stand on the spot in a state of abandonment, thereby enlisting her sympathy.

5

Arkadina redirects her annoyance at him by COM-
MANDING, thereby agreeing to act out the role of the
mother, but on her own terms. She moves forward and
takes command of the space and the proceedings.
Kostya obeys, happy to have her attention on any terms.

Arkadina's annoyance still hasn't been fully expiated,
so while addressing herself to the bandage she MOCKS
Kostya's appearance, RIDICULES the fact that other
people think he's a foreigner and finally, having
removed the bandage, BELITTLES the wound, making
it clear that she thinks he is making a fuss about nothing, and 'kisses the wound better' as mothers do with
their children's insignificant injuries.

5

Through all of this, Kostya presumably remains limp
and passive, which prompts Arkadina to use this
re-enacting of the mother-and-child relationship to
INFANTILISE him, implying that the act of shooting
himself was just a piece of childish clumsiness.

Kostya hears the jibe, but stays in the role of child,
meekly OBEYING but taking the opportunity to
SADDEN her with his own version of events in a way
that she can't ignore. He then REASSURES her, but the
point has been made. At this stage in the proceedings
he is unable to move, but he can make great use of his
helpless state, forcing her to deal gently with him. All
through the remaining actions in this long speech he is
presumably out of visual contact with her, and can only
gauge her reaction to him through her hands (since she
does not speak). The actor playing Arkadina will
therefore need to plot a series of *reactions* to Kostya
which can be communicated not just through the face
(because he can't see her face) but through touch.

When Kostya WORSHIPS her 'magic hands' (kissing one of them), this is presumably because she has responded in a maternal way to his sadness. As Kostya REMINDS her of their life together during his childhood she may respond further, and the physical fact of Kostya sitting passively like a child while she attends to him, makes the evocation all the more poignant. It may be that she slows or becomes gentler with the process of cleaning the wound, thereby revealing to him that she is affected. Possibly, being REMINDED of a time when she had more compassion and less vanity and being ADMIRED for it has a very palpable effect on her, and she may even break the physical contact in order not to betray those feelings.

Kostya, feeling her reaction, then NUDGES her for a response, perhaps turning to make eye contact. The eye contact and the nudge unnerve her and she perhaps turns his head back, EVADING him by starting the slightly brisker process of re-bandaging.

Unable to move or re-establish eye contact, Kostya can only verbally PROD her, using a more insistent tone to try and get her to acknowledge some part of their former life together. Arkadina's calm application of the fresh bandage is an expression of her control over the conversation. The subject of the two dancers is possibly more palatable to her because it doesn't make the same emotional appeal as the washerwoman story, so she MEETS him by briefly and non-committally acknowledging this memory.

Kostya then AMUSES her by remembering how religious the dancers were (perhaps surprising in the theatre world), but Arkadina doesn't respond, probably

5

because she has no use for such reminiscences. The bandage is almost on, and Kostya, experiencing her silence, presumably feels that his moment is slipping away, so he ADORES her as she fastens the bandage and then turns and CLINGS TO her to stop her moving away. Arkadina presumably allows this for a moment, then extricates herself to pack away the medical equipment, prompting Kostya to stand and REPROACH her.

Seeing an outburst coming, Arkadina REBUKES him in order to check his advance, then, not wishing to be in conflict with him, INSPIRES him to think differently about Trigorin, presumably moving towards him. Kostya wants contact with her, but not on these terms, so he CHALLENGES her, standing his ground but discouraging her attempt to inspire him. Arkadina turns away, and Kostya, wanting to force her to have this conversation, MOCKS her devotion to Trigorin, taking a backward step and raising his voice as if he doesn't care who hears him. Arkadina detects the childish provocation, but refuses to rise to it, continuing to pack the medical box and remaining calm. Having DERIDED and CORRECTED Kostya, Arkadina can then approach him to DISCIPLINE him, but he DEFIES her, walking away from her around the table and then RIDICULES her from a safe distance. Arkadina stops, refusing to engage in this pursuit, while Kostya, once again anxious that she will simply leave the room, quickly changes tack and comes towards her to AWAKEN her. Hearing his words, Arkadina turns away to shut him out, forcing him to NEEDLE her from behind. He succeeds in this, and she turns on him to EXPOSE his vindictiveness and SILENCE him.

As before when she used her maternal authority, Kostya DEFIES her, backing off and UNDERMINING from a distance, then returning to STAB her. Arkadina responds by standing her ground and REBUFFING him, then advancing on him to SCOLD, and finally MOCKING him with a wide hand gesture and walking off. Kostya then RIDICULES her by imitating her voice and BAITS her, stepping towards her but keeping a distance between them, then DESPISING her and finally stepping back and REJECTING her with a wave of his arm.

Arkadina SHAMES him with what is presumably meant to be an exit line, because Kostya then PROVOKES her in order to stop her having the last word and leaving the room. Unable to ignore the provocation, she returns to ATTACK him, and then, seeing his satisfaction at having riled her, she INSULTS him and when this doesn't work, PURSUES him. He retreats from her, ACCUSING, upon which she SLAPS him (maybe literally), causing him to weep and collapse into a chair. Disconcerted, Arkadina initially tries to SUPPRESS his tears from a distance, then goes in and PLEADS, before finally falling on her knees and BEGGING forgiveness. Having let go of her dignity and reserve, she is able to reveal her own unhappiness (about her own fading star and Trigorin's infidelity) and ENLIST his sympathy. Kostya EMBRACES her, but only to give himself licence to pour out his own woes (I MOVE) and force her to be a mother to him by ALARMING her that he might make another suicide attempt. Arkadina quickly recovers and extricates herself, ENCOURAGING him to cheer up, then standing up to REASSURE him that she is going very soon and taking Trigorin with her.

5

Kostya continues to cry, so she comes back, leans over him and hugs him until he stops, then STEADIES him, holding his head between her hands. He ACCEPTS her, taking her hands and kissing them. Arkadina uses the hand contact to raise him to standing position, COAXING him to be a grown-up, then holding his hands firmly to WARN him against fighting a duel.

Kostya realises that this is the best deal he is likely to get, and that Trigorin's absence is his best hope for winning back Nina, so he OBEYS her, dropping his hands submissively, then hugs her to ENTREAT her not to make him seek any kind of reconciliation with Trigorin. Finally he WORRIES her by sinking back into the chair and holding his bandaged head, to ensure that she makes no such demand.

It is quite possible, working alone, for you to establish a sequence of moves and gestures of this kind just by considering the given circumstances, character objectives and action verbs, but it is usually far more productive to do it in the rehearsal room, using your own impulses and ideas together with the demands and suggestions communicated by the action verbs to discover all the potential changes of direction and energy which take place as the characters react to one another.

The 'template' of physical moves thereby created is very different from traditional 'blocking', because it emerges from the action verbs themselves, which, of course, represent your own analysis of moments within the text. Each move is therefore designed to amplify and embody an intentional and reactive moment, defined by the action verb and expressed by the words of the text. What is important is not the precise nature of the moves themselves (although these have to be functional expressions of the action verbs) but the way in which you force each other to *energise into each reactive choice*. With a template like this, each thought-change is amplified into a strong physical and vocal shift, which allows you to experience both your own and the other actor's thought-changes as events rather than abstract concepts.

Within a complex psychological drama such as *The Seagull*, your task is to find clear and readable physical actions that encapsulate and clarify psychological moments within the dialogue. The complexity that the audience experiences does not arise from the ambiguity of any individual moment in the action, but in the rapid shift from one clear moment to the next.

5

Maintaining Connection

Despite the fact that the physical journey detailed in the last chapter is based on quite a detailed analysis of the relationship between the characters, there is still a danger, when you come to *play* your chosen actions and physical moves, that the scene could become 'mechanical', as you shift from one action to the next without necessarily connecting imaginatively and emotionally with each moment of the scene. To avoid this, and to deepen your connection to the backstory and character objective, there are two other techniques you can apply.

Unpacking the Action

At this stage of the Actioning process, especially with text as complex as this, it can often be useful, while exploring the physicality of the scene, to employ a technique which I call unpacking the action. This technique is designed to link the action verb directly back to the character objective, thereby helping the actor to understand the unique context and precise intention of each action verb, and of each physical move or gesture, within the overall need or desire driving the character through the play.

To unpack the action, you simply take one of your chosen action verbs, and ask why and to what end your character is playing that particular action in that precise moment. You can 'unpack' any action verb by simply extending the verb into a sentence, as in the example below:

> 'I CAJOLE you… into changing my bandage because this will get your attention and keep you beside me for a few minutes, thereby allowing me to say how I feel.'

The simple act of asking yourself why you are playing an action, and precisely what change you are trying to bring about in the other character, will have the effect of connecting you emotionally, physically and spatially to the other character. In an earlier chapter we investigated the notion that all actions are reactions. Here, by 'unpacking' the actions, we remind ourselves that all actions are also mini-intentions, pushing towards the overall scene objective.

Clearly there needs to be a very strong relationship between the moment-by-moment intentions driving each action verb, and the character's scene objective. This may seem very simple and obvious, but it is surprising how often actors forget to relate their action verbs back to the character objective, or even just to ask why their character is playing that particular action. By 'unpacking' each action you create a little fragment of your character's emotional and intentional 'narrative'.

In the table below I have 'unpacked' each action so that the 'story' of the scene is revealed from the action verbs themselves:

TEXT	ACTION VERB	'UNPACKING' THE VERB
K: Mother, will you change my bandage, please?	I CAJOLE…	you into changing my bandage because this will get your attention and keep you beside me for a few minutes, thereby allowing me to say how I feel.
K: You do it so well.	I COMPLIMENT…	you because I feel your resistance and I know you are susceptible to flattery.
A: The doctor's late.	I PUNISH…	you because I resent you 'pushing my buttons'.
K: He said he'd be here by ten, and it's already noon.	I ENLIST…	you to take away the feeling I have of being abandoned.
A: Sit down.	I COMMAND…	you because I'm angry with you for manipulating me and I want you to stop playing the child.
A: You look as if you're wearing a turban.	I MOCK…	you because you take yourself too seriously.
A: Someone came into the kitchen yesterday and asked what nationality you were.	I RIDICULE…	you because you didn't laugh at my joke and you need to know how ridiculous you look.
A: It's almost completely healed. Hardly anything left.	I BELITTLE…	you so that you will stop using your wound to manipulate me.
A: You won't fiddle around with guns again, will you, when I'm not here?	I INFANTILISE…	you so that you will get bored with playing the child and leave me alone.
K: No, Mother.	I OBEY…	you so that you will continue to mother me.
K: It was a moment of despair, sheer madness – I just couldn't control myself.	I SADDEN…	you so that you will want to protect me.
K: It won't happen again	I REASSURE…	you so that you won't get cross with me.
K: You have magic hands.	I WORSHIP…	you because I know you respond to adoration.
K: I remember a long time ago, when you were still acting in the State theatres – I was quite small then – and there was a fight in our yard, and one of the tenants, a washerwoman, got badly beaten.	I REMIND…	you about our former life together because I want you to remember how important I was to you.
K: She was unconscious when they picked her up… you kept going to see her, taking medicines to her, washing her children in the tub.	I ADMIRE…	you because I want you to keep listening and not switch off.

K: You don't remember?	I NUDGE...	you because you're not responding.
A: No.	I EVADE...	you because I don't want to become nostalgic and vulnerable.
K: There were two girls, ballet dancers, living in the same block. They used to drop in for coffee.	I PROD...	you because I want you to acknowledge that we share these memories.
A: Yes, that I do remember.	I MEET...	you because this is a less challenging memory and I don't want to upset you.
K: They were very religious.	I AMUSE...	you in order to relax you and get you chatting.
K: You know, these past few days, I've loved you just as tenderly and as devotedly as when I was a child.	I ADORE...	you because I want to force you into responding to me.
K: There's no one left for me now, except you.	I CLING TO...	you because I need you to respond to me.
K: But why, tell me why has this man come between us?	I REPROACH...	you because you haven't responded to me.
A: You don't understand him, Kostya.	I REBUKE...	you because you've used the intimacy of this moment to attack my lover.
A: He's a very noble character.	I INSPIRE...	you to admire Trigorin because that's the only way we can all co-exist.
K: Yes, and when he heard I was about to challenge him to a duel, his nobility didn't stop him taking the coward's way out.	I CHALLENGE...	you to face the truth about him, because I see how deluded you are.
K: He's leaving. Saving his skin!	I MOCK...	your gullibility because you can't see what a hollow man he is.
A: Oh, what rubbish!	I DERIDE...	your paranoid suppositions.
A: I'm taking him away myself.	I CORRECT...	your assumptions about Trigorin in order to bring you to your senses.
A: Kostya, you may not like our relationship, but you're an intelligent boy, and I have the right to demand that you respect my freedom.	I DISCIPLINE...	you because you're attempting to control me.
K: I respect your freedom, yes, but you must allow me my freedom to treat this man how I please.	I DEFY...	you to stop me thinking and speaking as I feel.
K: Noble character, huh!	I RIDICULE...	your delusions about Trigorin.

K: Look at us, we're practically falling out over him, and he's sitting right now in the drawing room or the garden somewhere, laughing at the pair of us…	I AWAKEN…	you to Trigorin's duplicity and infidelity in order to make you see sense.
K: working on Nina, trying to convince her he's a genius.	I NEEDLE…	you because you aren't reacting to me and you look as if you might leave the room.
A: You take a delight in being nasty to me.	I EXPOSE…	your malice as the childish jealousy it is.
A: I respect that man, and I'll ask you not to speak ill of him in my presence.	I SILENCE…	you because you're about to start deriding Trigorin again and you need a firm hand.
K: Well, I don't respect him.	I DEFY…	you because you need to know that you can't reject me one minute and control me the next.
K: You want me to think he's a genius, as you do, but I'm sorry, I can't lie,	I UNDERMINE…	you because you think I'm deluded and you need to know that you're the deluded one.
K: his writing just makes me sick.	I STAB…	you in order to shock you into a realisation of Trigorin's worthlessness.
A: That's pure envy.	I REBUFF…	you because you're completely out of control and need stopping.
A: People with no talent, but plenty of pretension – that's all they can do, run down genuine talent.	I SCOLD…	you for openly criticising Trigorin's writing by making you realise that until you can do better you have no right to carp.
A: Well that's scant consolation, I'd say.	I MOCK…	you for running down published writers to make your own failure feel better.
K: Genuine talent!	I RIDICULE…	you for your lack of discrimination.
K: If it comes to that, I've got more talent than the whole lot of you!	I BAIT…	you into attacking me so that you'll feel guilty.
K: You people with your stale conventions, you've got the art world in your pocket, you think what you do is the only legitimate real work, everything else you try to stifle and suppress!	I DESPISE…	your narrow conventional view of art which makes you admire Trigorin and dismiss my work.
K: Well, I don't acknowledge you! I don't acknowledge either you or him!	I REJECT…	you and your lover so you'll understand it's him or me.
A: Decadent!…	I SHAME…	you for placing your naive amateur pretensions above professional work.

K: Go back to your cosy little theatre and act in your pathetic, rubbishy plays!	I PROVOKE...	you with the lack of vision or true understanding of the world within your work.
A: I've never acted in rubbish. Leave me alone!	I ATTACK...	you for trying to undermine everything that I've fought for in my life.
A: You couldn't even write a third-rate farce.	I INSULT...	you because you need putting down.
A: Provincial philistine! Sponger!	I PURSUE...	you because you aren't listening.
K: Miser!	I ACCUSE...	you of keeping me short of money and imprisoning me on your brother's estate.
A: Tramp! Nonentity!	I SLAP...	you for your ingratitude.
A: Look, don't cry. There's no need for that.	I SUPPRESS...	your grief because it pains me.
A: Don't, please.	I PLEAD WITH...	you to stop crying because I feel so guilty and I'm afraid you'll use that against me.
A: Oh, my darling boy, forgive me, please. Forgive your sinful mother.	I BEG...	you to forgive me so that you'll understand my weakness and stop pressurising me.
A: Forgive me, I'm so unhappy.	I ENLIST...	you to pity my unhappiness and realise that I'm already in pain.
K: Oh, if only you knew!	I EMBRACE...	you to make you feel close to me and understand my pain.
K: I've lost everything. She doesn't love me, I can't write any more.	I MOVE...	you to sympathy for my situation with Nina so that you'll want to do something for me.
K: I've nothing left to live for.	I ALARM...	you because I know you're scared I'll try to kill myself again.
A: Don't give up hope. It'll all turn out right.	I ENCOURAGE...	you because I want you to cheer up and stop burdening me with your self-pity.
A: I'm taking him away now, she'll come to love you again.	I REASSURE...	you that Trigorin's not a problem, so you won't make any more demands.
A: Don't cry.	I IMPLORE...	you to stop crying because I hate the way it makes me feel.
A: We're friends again, right?	I STEADY...	you so you'll let me go without making me feel guilty.
K: Yes, Mother.	I ACCEPT...	you because I don't want you to reject me again.

A: Kostya, make it up with him.	I COAX…	you to speak to Trigorin because I don't want to have to choose between you.
A: We don't want any duels, do we.	I WARN…	you against challenging Trigorin to a duel because it would frighten him away.
K: All right.	I OBEY…	you because you have shown you do love me and Trigorin is going.
K: Only please don't make me face him. That's too hard.	I ENTREAT…	you not to make me speak to Trigorin because I don't want to stop hating him.
K: I haven't the strength…	I WORRY…	you with the fact I'm still in a very unstable state, in order to make you back off.

'Unpacking' the action is a relatively simple but very useful technique for ensuring that every action played is not only reactive to the other characters, but also connected to the subtext and consistent with the logic of the story. By asking yourself *why* your character plays each action and precisely what he hopes to gain from it, you can ensure that every action is 'powered' by the emotional energy of the scene objective, the super-objective and the character's understanding of his situation. What is more, your attention will be continually focused on the other actor, as your character seeks to achieve one mini-objective after another, and to bend the other character to his will.

Having 'unpacked' each action verb and understood the intentional context in which each action verb might be played, it can be very useful to do an exercise in which you and your scene partner play the scene speaking *only* the action verbs and an improvised version of the 'unpacking', so that a new subtextual dialogue emerges. This exercise not only helps to 'peg' each action verb to its intentional context within your own mind, but it also alerts your scene partner to the level of your character's need,

6

and you to theirs, thereby raising the stakes and making both of you more aware of the conflict between the characters and the manipulative power they have over one another.

Resonators

Another simple but effective technique you can use to connect imaginatively and emotionally with the text is to plot resonators into the backstory, to which each action verb can be connected. A resonator can be defined as a significant memory of a moment in a character's past which, if linked to a line of text, can make the words resonate with the emotional energy of that memory. Resonators can be either moments from the play itself, or moments which are mentioned in the text, or even imagined moments in the character's life which are consistent with the main backstory but have a particular poignancy of their own. Sometimes the resonators will be self-evident; at other times you may have to use your imagination to create incidents within the backstory that have the power to heighten and intensify a line of text.

In the table below I have 'plotted' a series of possible resonators, some taken directly from the play itself and some constructed from the character backstories.

TEXT	ACTION VERB	'UNPACKING' THE VERB	RESONATOR
…: Mother, will you change my bandage, please?	I CAJOLE…	you into changing my bandage because this will get your attention and keep you beside me for a few minutes, thereby allowing me to say how I feel.	An incident in Kostya's childhood when he fell over, grazed his knee, and was nursed tenderly by his mother.
…: You do it so well.	I COMPLIMENT…	you because I feel your resistance and I know you are susceptible to flattery.	An incident in Kostya's childhood when he witnessed her responding to male flattery.
…: The doctor's late.	I PUNISH…	you because I resent you 'pushing my buttons'.	An evening when Arkadina was entertaining a male friend, and the child Kostya kept appearing in the doorway saying he couldn't sleep.
…: He said he'd be here by ten, and it's already noon.	I ENLIST…	you to take away the feeling I have of being abandoned.	The first time that Arkadina left Kostya alone all night.
…: Sit down.	I COMMAND…	you because I'm angry with you for manipulating me and I want you to stop playing the child.	A night when Kostya wouldn't stop crying until Arkadina got so angry she shouted at him.
…: You look as if you're wearing a turban.	I MOCK…	you because you take yourself too seriously.	The performance of Kostya's play in Act One.
…: Someone came into the kitchen yesterday and asked what nationality you were.	I RIDICULE…	you because you didn't laugh at my joke and you need to know how ridiculous you look.	As above.
…: It's almost completely healed. Hardly anything left.	I BELITTLE…	you so that you will stop using your wound to manipulate me.	An incident in Kostya's childhood when he fell over and hurt himself slightly but screamed for ages.
…: You won't fiddle around with buns again, will you, when I'm not here?	I INFANTILISE…	you so that you will get bored with playing the child and leave me alone.	As above.
…: No, Mother.	I OBEY…	you so that you will continue to mother me.	An incident in Kostya's childhood when he became scared in the night and Arkadina held his hand till he went to sleep.
…: It was a moment of despair, sheer madness – I just couldn't control myself.	I SADDEN…	you so that you will want to protect me.	As above.
…: It won't happen again.	I REASSURE…	you so that you won't get cross with me.	As above.
…: You have magic hands.	I WORSHIP…	you because I know you respond to adoration.	The first time Kostya saw his mother in a play.
…: I remember a long time ago, when you were still acting in the State theatres – I was quite small then – and there was a fight in our yard, and one of the tenants, a washerwoman, got badly beaten.	I REMIND…	you about our former life together because I want you to remember how important I was to you.	The memory as described.
…: She was unconscious when they picked her up… you kept going to see her, taking medicines to her, washing her children in the tub.	I ADMIRE…	you because I want you to keep listening and not switch off.	As above.

K: You don't remember?	I NUDGE…	you because you're not responding.	As above.
A: No.	I EVADE…	you because I don't want to become nostalgic and vulnerable.	As above.
K: There were two girls, ballet dancers, living in the same block. They used to drop in for coffee.	I PROD…	you because I want you to acknowledge that we share these memories.	The memory as described.
A: Yes, that I do remember.	I MEET…	you because this is a less challenging memory and I don't want to upset you.	As above.
K: They were very religious.	I AMUSE…	you in order to relax you and get you chatting.	A moment when Arkadina was rebuked by one of the dancers for washing clothes on a Sunday.
K: You know, these past few days, I've loved you just as tenderly and as devotedly as when I was a child.	I ADORE…	you because I want to force you into responding to me.	Kostya smelling his mother's perfume as she kissed him goodbye before heading off to the theatre.
K: There's no one left for me now, except you.	I CLING TO…	you because I need you to respond to me.	As above.
K: But why, tell me why has this man come between us?	I REPROACH…	you because you haven't responded to me.	The first time Arkadina let a man stay the night in her bedroom and Kostya had to sleep on the sofa.
A: You don't understand him, Kostya.	I REBUKE…	you because you've used the intimacy of this moment to attack my lover.	A lover who abandoned Arkadina because he couldn't deal with Kostya.
A: He's a very noble character.	I INSPIRE…	you to admire Trigorin because that's the only way we can all co-exist.	As above.
K: Yes, and when he heard I was about to challenge him to a duel, his nobility didn't stop him taking the coward's way out.	I CHALLENGE…	you to face the truth about him, because I see how deluded you are.	The scene described.
K: He's leaving. Saving his skin!	I MOCK…	your gullibility because you can't see what a hollow man he is.	As above.
A: Oh, what rubbish!	I DERIDE…	your paranoid suppositions.	A time in Kostya's childhood when he was convinced there was a monster under the bed and wouldn't go to sleep.
A: I'm taking him away myself.	I CORRECT…	your assumptions about Trigorin in order to bring you to your senses.	As above.
A: Kostya, you may not like our relationship, but you're an intelligent boy, and I have the right to demand that you respect my freedom.	I DISCIPLINE…	you because you're attempting to control me.	As above.
K: I respect your freedom, yes, but you must allow me my freedom to treat this man how I please.	I DEFY…	you to stop me thinking and speaking as I feel.	An incident in Kostya's childhood when he was rude to one of Arkadina's lovers, who then slapped him.
K: Noble character, huh!	I RIDICULE…	your delusions about Trigorin.	As above.

Look at us, we're practically lling out all over him, and he's sitting ght now in the drawing room or e garden somewhere, laughing at e pair of us...	I AWAKEN...	you to Trigorin's duplicity and infidelity in order to make you see sense.	An incident in Kostya's child-hood when one of Arkadina's lovers stole money from her and fled the following morning.
: working on Nina, trying to onvince her he's a genius.	I NEEDLE...	you because you aren't reacting to me and you look as if you might leave the room.	As above.
: You take a delight in being asty to me.	I EXPOSE...	your malice as the childish jealousy it is.	An incident in Kostya's child-hood when he smashed a favourite vase of hers in anger.
: I respect that man, and I'll sk you not to speak ill of him my presence.	I SILENCE...	you because you're about to start deriding Trigorin again and you need a firm hand.	As above.
: Well, I don't respect him.	I DEFY...	you because you need to know that you can't reject me one minute and control me the next.	An incident in Kostya's child-hood when he was rude to one of Arkadina's lovers, who then slapped him.
You want me to think he's a enius, as you do, but I'm sorry, can't lie,	I UNDERMINE...	you because you think I'm deluded and you need to know that you're the deluded one.	As above.
: his writing just makes me ck.	I STAB...	you in order to shock you into a realisation of Trigorin's worthlessness.	As above.
: That's pure envy.	I REBUFF...	you because you're completely out of control and need stopping.	An incident in Kostya's child-hood when he smashed a favourite vase of hers in anger.
People with no talent, but enty of pretension – that's all ey can do, run down genuine lent.	I SCOLD...	you for openly criticising Trigorin's writing by making you realise that until you can do better you have no right to carp.	The performance of Kostya's play in Act One.
Well that's scant consolation, I say.	I MOCK...	you for running down published writers to make your own failure feel better.	As above.
Genuine talent!	I RIDICULE...	you for your lack of discrimination.	A memory of a truly dreadful melodrama that Arkadina acted in when Kostya was fifteen.
If it comes to that, I've got ore talent than the whole lot you!	I BAIT...	you into attacking me so that you'll feel guilty.	As above.
You people with your stale con-ntions, you've got the art world in ur pocket, you think what you do the only legitimate real work, erything else you try to stifle and ppress!	I DESPISE...	your narrow conventional view of art which makes you admire Trigorin and dismiss my work.	As above.
Well, I don't acknowledge u! I don't acknowledge either u or him!	I REJECT...	you and your lover so you'll understand it's him or me.	A memory of Arkadina's openly mocking reaction to the performance in Act One, and Trigorin's ironic silence.
Decadent!...	I SHAME...	you for placing your naive amateur pretensions above professional work.	A sense of empathy with Nina for having her desire to act exploited by a bad writer's ego.

K: Go back to your cosy little theatre and act in your pathetic, rubbishy plays!	I PROVOKE…	you with the lack of vision or true understanding of the world within your work.	A memory of a truly dreadful melodrama that Arkadina acted in when Kostya was fifteen.
A: I've never acted in rubbish. Leave me alone!	I ATTACK…	you for trying to undermine everything that I've fought for in my life.	A memory of the same play, and the shame she felt when artists she respected came to see it.
A: You couldn't even write a third-rate farce.	I INSULT…	you because you need putting down.	As above.
A: Provincial philistine! Sponger!	I PURSUE…	you because you aren't listening.	An incident when a theatre manager offered the teenage Kostya work as a stagehand, but he refused.
K: Miser!	I ACCUSE…	you of keeping me short of money and imprisoning me on your brother's estate.	An incident when Kostya discovered Arkadina's hidden savings, shortly after she had refused to buy him a new overcoat.
A: Tramp! Nonentity!	I SLAP…	you for your ingratitude.	An incident when Kostya brought a group of shabbily dressed bohemian friends back to the apartment.
A: Look, don't cry. There's no need for that.	I SUPPRESS…	your grief because it pains me.	A very similar moment in Kostya's childhood when she lost her temper, hit him, and felt immediately guilty because he cried so inconsolably.
A: Don't, please.	I PLEAD WITH…	you to stop crying because I feel so guilty and I'm afraid you'll use that against me.	As above.
A: Oh, my darling boy, forgive me, please. Forgive your sinful mother.	I BEG…	you to forgive me so that you'll understand my weakness and stop pressurising me.	As above.
A: Forgive me, I'm so unhappy.	I ENLIST…	you to pity my unhappiness and realise that I'm already in pain.	The moment when Arkadina first saw Trigorin talking to Nina.
K: Oh, if only you knew!	I EMBRACE…	you to make you feel close to me and understand my pain.	The incident with the seagull in Act Two.
K: I've lost everything. She doesn't love me, I can't write any more.	I MOVE…	you to sympathy for my situation with Nina so that you'll want to do something for me.	As above.
K: I've nothing left to live for.	I ALARM…	you because I know you're scared I'll try to kill myself again.	As above.
A: Don't give up hope. It'll all turn out right.	I ENCOURAGE…	you because I want you to cheer up and stop burdening me with your self-pity.	An incident when Kostya as a child cried inconsolably for hours.
A: I'm taking him away now, she'll come to love you again.	I REASSURE…	you that Trigorin's not a problem, so you won't make any more demands.	As above.
A: Don't cry.	I IMPLORE…	you to stop crying because I hate the way it makes me feel.	As above.
A: We're friends again, right?	I STEADY…	you so you'll let me go without making me feel guilty.	As above.
K: Yes, mother.	I ACCEPT…	you because I don't want you to reject me again.	An incident where Arkadina hit Kostya as a child and then begged his forgiveness.

A: Kostya, make it up with him.	I COAX…	you to speak to Trigorin because I don't want to have to choose between you.	An incident when Kostya as a child was so rude to one of Arkadina's gentlemen friends that he walked out in fury.
A: We don't want any duels, do we.	I WARN…	you against challenging Trigorin to a duel because it would frighten him away.	An incident where Kostya got into a fight in the yard and was soundly beaten.
K: All right.	I OBEY…	you because you have shown you do love me and Trigorin is going.	As previously, an incident where Arkadina hit Kostya as a child and then begged his forgiveness.
K: Only please don't make me face him. That's too hard.	I ENTREAT…	you not to make me speak to Trigorin because I don't want to stop hating him.	As above.
K: I haven't the strength…	I WORRY…	you with the fact I'm still in a very unstable state, in order to make you back off.	As above.

The process of identifying, fleshing-out and adopting these resonator moments so that they become the character's 'memories' is usually a highly creative and enjoyable one. As you engage your creative imagination to give colour and poignancy to these mini-narratives, you will inject into the character the 'lifeblood' of your own human experience and emotional understanding, thereby establishing an indissoluble bond between you and the character.

6

The relationship between the resonators and the character backstory is actually a reciprocal one. Most actors write their backstory quite early in the rehearsal process, using a mixture of textual 'facts' and conjecture to fill in the gaps. Once you have started to investigate the text in rehearsal, and to plot in your resonators, you may realise that there are additional narrative elements that you want to include in the backstory, in order to find a fuller connection to moments within the play itself. For this reason, the backstory should always be a flexible document that may be changed or added to as your investigations proceed.

Resonators based on events in the play can be easily explored through rehearsal, but those that are based in the conjectural backstory usually need to be investigated further in order for you to find a stronger connection. Techniques you can use include:

- Improvisation of the 'resonator scene' in the backstory. As part of the rehearsal process you can play out a scene through improvisation with other members of the cast, usually two or three times until it is firmly fixed in your memory, and forms part of your character history.

- Writing a diary entry or account of the incident, or a letter immediately after the incident.

- Having an improvised conversation with another member of the cast (in this case the actor playing Konstantin might use Sorin, Dorn, Nina or even Masha) in which the story of the incident is told in a very detailed way that includes facts and feelings.

The key issue here is that action verbs and their associated physical gestures/moves should always inform, and be informed by, the actor's understanding of the play, the relationships and the character objective – they should never be seen in isolation as a template for playing a role. The clarity offered by action verbs and physical choices can connect you to the 'moment of doing' and offer you a distillation of thought and feeling, but you, the actor, have to make the connection back to the given circumstances and to the story you are telling, and embody those things, otherwise your actions will ultimately be empty and devoid of humanity.

Above all, resonators should seek to bring together and make *useful and specific* all the research and reflective thinking you have done to support your work on character, such as backstory, character research, vocal/physical transformation and textual analysis. Doing this exercise will help you make clear connections between your Stanislavsky-based investigations and specific moments in the text. Most actors have no problem sifting a text for information and writing a character backstory, but most find it more difficult to 'own' that backstory in the space – by which I mean allowing the significant experiences and events contained in the backstory to influence and affect moments of reaction and impulse on stage, just as they do in real life. While no actor can ever completely 'own' the character backstory in the way that a real person owns their life story, you can at least make the backstory more vivid, specific and affective by 'pegging' lines of text to specific memories in your character's fictional life.

6

Signposting

In Chapters Three and Four we investigated ways in which the actor can resist the temptation to play every action as a 'forward action' (i.e. constantly moving towards the target of their action verbs) by using the possibilities of a changing physical/spatial dynamic rather than constant physical proximity.

In drawing our 'floor plans' of moves, and exploring gesture and touch, we have discovered that many actions can best be played by actually *increasing* the physical distance between characters, or by otherwise altering the spatial dynamic (e.g. sitting down or standing up). This awareness of space as a factor within the relationship allows you to think and make decisions in three dimensions rather than the single dimension of a straight line between you and your scene partner.

7

In Chapter Six, we also looked at alternative focal points provided by the resonators embedded in the backstory. By virtue of their location in the character's past, the resonators help you to imagine your character living on a genuine timeline of memory, change and expectation. Although these focal points exist only in the imagination, they create a 'triangulation' between your character, the other character and the moment in the past that informs this moment. This adds a further dimension – time – to the imaginative landscape.

In this chapter we will be looking at yet another triangulation, which covers the literal space, the conjectural space (i.e. the world beyond that which is visible), and a timeline that potentially stretches from the distant past into the future. We call this 'signposting', and for the actor it is an invaluable tool in discovering the character's psychophysical journey.

Signposting starts with the notion that every textual 'thought' (with its associated action verb) is by definition attempting to *draw the attention* of your scene partner towards some concrete or abstract 'thing'. That something could be tangible and present, as in: 'oh look, the clock's stopped', or it could exist elsewhere in time and/or space, as in: 'I loved her, you know.' The act of drawing your scene partner's attention to whatever it is you want them to see or understand forms an integral and essential part of playing each action verb, the idea being that if you can get the other character to see, either literally or imaginatively, what your character sees, then they will be convinced or changed in the way intended.

In the following passage from Act Two of *Three Sisters* by Anton Chekhov, Natasha, a girl born and bred in the remote provincial town where the play is set, has married Andrei Prozorov, brother of Olga, Masha and Irina, and the only son of the late General Prozorov, former commander of the garrison stationed in the town. At this point in the play they have been married for nearly two years and have a young son, Bobik. However, they have nothing in common, and Andrei divides his time between reading in his bedroom and gambling at a local casino with Chebutykin, the army doctor who lodges downstairs.

Natasha meanwhile has begun an affair with Protopopov, a powerful local businessman who was her suitor before her marriage. She has also embarked on the project of ejecting Andrei's sisters from their family home, something she finally achieves at the end of Act Four.

At the start of Act Two, it is carnival time, and there is to be a party at the house, to which a number of army officers are invited. As in past years, a group of musicians is also due to arrive at 10 p.m. However, Natasha has had an invitation from Protopopov to go out with him in his troika, and she has therefore set about cancelling the party (without revealing her real reasons) so that the coast will be clear by the time Protopopov arrives. Her excuse is that little Bobik is ill and will be disturbed by the music and dancing. Her obstacle is that the party is a long-standing tradition in the Prozorov house, and Andrei is reluctant to cancel it without his sisters' permission.

Andrei, on the other hand, has the slightly weaker objective of wanting her to go away and leave him in peace. His obstacle is that she clearly wants him to agree to making controversial changes in the house as the price of her absence.

7

It is eight o'clock in the evening. Offstage, an accordion is being played outside, faintly audible. The room is unlit. NATASHA enters in her dressing gown, holding a candle. She crosses the stage and pauses at the door leading to ANDREI's room.

NATASHA. Andrei, / what are you doing? / You're reading? / Oh, it doesn't matter, I was just wondering… / (She moves on, opens another door, looks in, then closes it.) No lights left on…

ANDREI (emerging with a book in his hand). What is it, Natasha?

NATASHA. I'm checking to see if there's a light on… / It's carnival time, the servants are getting careless, / you have to keep an eye on them constantly, to make sure nothing's wrong. / I walked through the dining room at midnight last night, and there was a candle left burning. / And I still haven't found out who lit it. (*She sets down the candle*). / What time is it?

ANDREI (*looks at his watch*). Quarter past eight.

NATASHA. And Olga and Irina still aren't in. They haven't come home. / They're kept busy the whole time, poor things. Olga at her staff meeting, Irina at her telegraph office… / (*Sighs.*) I said that to your sister this morning, 'You must look after yourself, Irina darling,' I said. But she doesn't listen. / Quarter past eight, did you say? / You know, I'm afraid our little Bobik isn't at all well. / Why is he so cold? He had a fever yesterday, and today he's freezing… / I'm really worried about him!

ANDREI. He's fine, Natasha. The boy's fine.

NATASHA. Still, we'd better see he's eating properly. / I'm worried. / And there's supposed to be carnival people arriving at ten o'clock, / I'd rather they didn't come, Andryusha.

ANDREI. Well, I don't know… After all, we did invite them.

NATASHA. You know, that darling little boy woke up this morning and looked at me, and he suddenly smiled – yes, he recognised me. 'Hello, Bobik!' I said, 'Hello, my darling!' And he laughed, yes. / Children know everything that's going on, they understand perfectly. / Anyway, Andryusha, I'll tell them not to let the musicians in.

ANDREI (*indecisively*). Well, that's surely up to my sisters. I mean, it's their house…

NATASHA. Yes, of course, I'll tell them too. They're so kind… / (*Makes to leave.*) I've ordered sour milk for supper. / The doctor says you're to have nothing but sour milk, otherwise you'll never lose weight.

As usual, we start by dividing this short passage into thoughts and identifying the action verb for each thought. We then try to identify precisely what, with each action verb, the characters are trying to 'signpost' for the other.

TEXT	ACTION VERB	SIGNPOSTING
N: Andrei,	I DISTURB	her own presence.
N: what are you doing?	I PROBE	Andrei's quiet inactivity.
N: You're reading?	I RESPECT	Andrei's intellectual superiority.
N: Oh, it doesn't matter, I was just wondering…	I PLACATE	her own unimportance.
N: No lights left on…	I DISTRACT	the drawing room and ballroom beyond.
A: What is it, Natasha?	I CHALLENGE	her obvious desire to say something.
N: I'm checking to see if there's a light on…	I REDIRECT	the rest of the house.
N: It's carnival time, the servants are getting careless,	I ALERT	the challenges of running a house.
N: you have to keep an eye on them constantly, to make sure nothing's wrong.	I WORRY	the poor quality of the servants.
N: I walked through the dining room at midnight last night, and there was a candle left burning.	I ALARM	the dining room last night.
N: And I still haven't found out who lit it.	I WARN	the continued presence of the culprit.
N: What time is it?	I QUIZ	Andrei's watch.
A. Quarter past eight.	I SATISFY	the time.

N: And Olga and Irina still aren't iN: They haven't come home.	I PERTURB	the absence of the sisters.
N: They're kept busy the whole time, poor things. Olga at her staff meeting, Irina at her telegraph office…	I DISCONCERT	the school and the telegraph office.
N: I said that to your sister this morning, 'You must look after yourself, Irina darling,' I said. But she doesn't listen.	I GALVANISE	the conversation she had with Irina that morning.
N: Quarter past eight, did you say?	I QUESTION	Andrei's watch.
N: You know, I'm afraid our little Bobik isn't at all well.	I UNNERVE	Bobik in his bed upstairs.
N: Why is he so cold? He had a fever yesterday, and today he's freezing…	I DISTRESS	as above.
N: I'm really worried about him!	I ENLIST	her own worry and stress.
A: He's fine, Natasha. The boy's fine.	I REASSURE	Bobik in his cot upstairs.
N: Still, we'd better see he's eating properly.	I RALLY	the nanny in Bobik's nursery.
N: I'm worried.	I UNSETTLE	the effect that the worry is having on her nerves.
N: And there's supposed to be carnival people arriving at ten o'clock,	I PANIC	the musicians (one of whom can be heard outside) and guests coming from the town.
N: I'd rather they didn't come, Andryusha.	I COERCE	the relative peace and calm in the house.
A: Well, I don't know… After all, we did invite them.	I RESIST	the musicians and guests.
N: You know, that darling little boy woke up this morning and looked at me, and he suddenly smiled – yes, he recognised me. 'Hello, Bobik!' I said, 'Hello, my darling!' And he laughed, yes.	I CHARM	Bobik in his cot upstairs.
N: Children know everything that's going on, they understand perfectly.	I WARN	Andrei's failure to put Bobik first.
N: Anyway, Andryusha, I'll tell them not to let the musicians in.	I OVERRIDE	the housemaid.
A: Well that's surely up to my sisters. I mean, it's their house…	I OPPOSE	Olga and Irina.

N: Yes, of course, I'll tell them too. They're so kind.	I SIDESTEP	Olga and Irina.
N: I've ordered sour milk for supper.	I PUNISH	The dining room.
N: The doctor says you're to have nothing but sour milk, otherwise you'll never lose weight.	I CONTROL	Andrei's excess weight.

Once you have identified precisely what your character is signposting on each thought, you can then do an exercise in which you play the scene by quite literally gesturing and/or moving towards the thing that you are signposting on each line. The precise nature of these gestures is entirely up to you. Your job as the actor is to generate an imaginary picture of what your character would like the other character to see or understand, to place that picture somewhere in the spatial world, and to find a physical and/or vocal gesture that directs the other actor towards it.

In preparation for this you will first need to undertake an essential process for any acting company, which is to *locate yourself geographically* within the world of the play. In the case of this particular play, you should, within the early stages of rehearsal, have agreed on a map of the town, including all the places mentioned in the text, and have set the location of the Prozorov house within it. You should also have decided in which direction the house faces, and created a plan of the rooms within the house.

Natasha's first 'signpost' is towards her own presence. The fact that the door is probably closed or partly closed forces her to DISTURB him, because she can't know otherwise whether he is there or what he is doing. As Andrei probably can't see her yet, there is little point in her literally gesturing towards herself (though she might do so anyway), but signposting doesn't always have to be a physical thing – if you are thinking about the signpost as you speak a line, this can change the quality of your voice accordingly.

The second action, I PROBE, shifts the signpost to Andrei himself, with particular reference to the lack of sound or movement in his room. To Natasha, who is constantly on the move and constantly talking, this level of silence and inactivity invites disturbance and enquiry. Again, since she probably can't see Andrei, there will be no physical gesture, but the shift in her focus from herself to Andrei will once again reveal itself through the vocal gesture.

Once visual contact has been established, which probably happens between the second and third actions, Natasha's gestures can start to become more physical. Her third action is I RESPECT. It is doubtful whether Natasha actually has any respect at all for reading or any other intellectual pursuit, yet in this particular situation it is arguably in her interests a) to placate Andrei and get him on side, and b) to ensure that he stays in his room. Her signposting of Andrei's intellectual superiority will most probably be conveyed through a slightly deferential tone and gesture.

The next action, I PLACATE, which is presumably a response to Andrei's evident annoyance at being disturbed, signposts Natasha's own relative unimportance. She could signpost this through a little self-mocking laugh and self-effacing body language. By playing low status she attempts to draw attention away from her objective (to get the dance cancelled), and make her disturbing him seem inconsequential. To reinforce this impression she immediately signposts the rest of the room with I DISTRACT, turning the subject to the household matter of servants leaving candles burning.

Andrei is not fooled, however. He knows her well enough to be aware that she always has a reason for her actions, and he CHALLENGES her, signposting her obvious desire to say something. This could be a clear and literal physical gesture towards her artificial body language.

Natasha, however, does not want to reveal her motivations yet, and she REDIRECTS his attention towards the darkened rooms of the house. Although she does this initially as a way of distracting him, she then uses this distraction to make the point that she is the only person keeping control of the house, signposting the challenges of running a large establishment (I ALERT), the fecklessness of servants (I WORRY) and the risk of fire in the dining room (I ALARM). All of these things, whether immediately visible or not, can be the subject of literal body and hand gestures, not least because Natasha is seeking to make and reinforce her point as strongly as possible. These last three action verbs, because of what they are signposting, could be played with three very different gestures. I ALERT might be a broad gesture covering the whole house; I WORRY relates to the servants' quarters and could therefore be a much more specific gesture; while I ALARM might pinpoint the exact location of the lighted candle Natasha claims to have found previously. I WARN could signpost the whole house again, but this time as a potentially dangerous place full of feckless people needing constant supervision.

At this point it is likely that Natasha detects Andrei's growing impatience and scepticism with her fears and preoccupations, so she deftly signposts his watch with I QUIZ. Andrei's only desire at this point is to SATISFY her and get rid of her, so he signposts his watch too. (You might of course choose I GALVANISE rather than I SATISFY as the action verb here, in which case Andrei would signpost Natasha's state of undress, reminding her that the party is due to begin relatively soon and she needs to go and get ready, but there is no indication in the text that this is the case.)

As ever, Natasha manages to turn the conversation to her own ends, signposting the absence of Olga and Irina, both of whom work long hours and are rarely present in the house (I PERTURB). This serves both Natasha's short-term and long-term objectives, since, as the only constant presence in the house, it would presumably make sense for her to be given complete authority. Natasha follows this up by signposting the sisters' respective workplaces (with a clear knowledge of their location in the town) and the excessive work-loads they both have (I DISCONCERT), the implication being that the sisters have enough to do without worrying about matters of household man-agement. She then tops this by implying that Irina is making herself ill with overwork and GALVANISING Andrei into intervening. For this action she signposts the exact location of the conversation with Irina that apparently took place that morning, thereby adding the ring of truth to what is most probably a total invention.

Suspecting that Andrei is losing patience, Natasha once again signposts his watch (I QUESTION), not because she has forgotten what the time is, but because she doesn't want to give Andrei any chance to argue with her. She then swiftly moves the conversation to the subject of Bobik (I UNNERVE followed by I DISTRESS), signposting the nursery upstairs. Seeing Andrei's doubt, she signposts her own worry (I ENLIST). Andrei responds by also signposting the nursery (where all is clearly peaceful) and REASSURING her. Natasha counters by signposting the nanny (who she implies is not competent to care for Bobik) and RALLYING him to pay more attention to his child. Seeing his reluctance, she once again signposts herself, UNSETTLING him with her anxiety. As if suddenly remembering, she PANICS him with the idea of the musicians and guests arriving for a party and keeping Bobik awake all night, signposting the music that can be heard outside. Finally she COERCES Andrei into cancelling the party, signposting the quiet house which is clearly ideal for Bobik's rest and recovery.

Taken aback, Andrei also signposts the musicians and guests, RESISTING her by pointing out the numbers of people who would be disappointed by the cancellation. Natasha then changes tack, CHARMING Andrei by signposting his little boy upstairs and then WARNING him by signposting his weakness and indecision, implying that Bobik will very quickly detect his father's lack of devotion.

Seizing the moment, Natasha then OVERRIDES Andrei, signposting the housemaid who would normally let the guests in. Andrei, unable to stand up to her himself, signposts Olga and Irina, OPPOSING her with the prospect of their displeasure. Natasha SIDESTEPS this by mirroring his signpost, to show that she

7

is quite happy to take the sisters on herself. Finally she PUNISHES him for failing to support her, signposting the inadequate supper she has ordered for him, and CONTROLS him by invoking doctor's orders and signposting his excess weight. This assertion of her authority is presumably designed to put him in his place and distract him from the issue of the party, yet as always, it is flimsily disguised as care and concern.

In the early stages of exploring signposting, it is important merely to try and physically locate everything that you are speaking about, so that you are completely clear where, whether on or off stage, each person, place or abstract idea is situated. To begin with it is fine to signpost through quite mechanical hand, body and vocal gestures, just in order to allow your body to understand the geographical journey of your character's focus as the scene progresses. These gestures, however, must always have reference to the other character, so that, just as a tour guide will make continual eye contact with the tourist while gesturing towards whatever she wants the tourist to see, so you the actor can allow your body to signpost something while your actual attention moves back and forth between the subject of your action verb and the subject of the 'signpost'.

One of the effects you may notice from this is that, as your body moves from one signpost to another, your voice will make reciprocal shifts, so that, for example, if you are signposting a room on the next floor up, as Natasha does in this scene, your voice may rise in pitch, while if the signpost is to something far away, your voice may take on a different resonance as if reaching across that distance.

You may also find that your body, rather than wanting to move towards your scene partner, now wants to move towards the subject of the signpost, although the need to achieve your objective with the other character keeps you from moving too far away, almost as if you were fastened to them with an invisible piece of elastic! Once again, there is a 'triangulation' between your character, the other character and the object of the signpost which keeps your body in relationship to the fictional space and the fictional world beyond, stimulating impulse and rooting your imagination within the given circumstances.

It is very important, once you are clear about all the different things you want to signpost, that you allow the body to find its own way of gesturing, otherwise you will get stuck with external and disconnected movements that do not have any intentional energy. The key question that you need to ask and keep asking is: 'can this other person actually understand and imagine what I am telling him?' This question is actually quite a familiar one to most of us, because there are many occasions in our lives when we have to describe something to another person so that they can see/experience it imaginatively as vividly as we experienced it in real life. To achieve this we use all kinds of gestures, and we watch our auditor constantly for signs of understanding and recognition – signs that inform us whether our words and gestures are evoking in them the kind of reciprocal imaginative response we are looking for.

Moving from one clear gesture to another by shifting the signposting is also one of the best ways for you to understand each thought and to locate it within the world of the play. Actioning in any case helps you to break up longer speeches into different intentional moments, but signposting helps you discover the physical dimension of each thought-change through clear and precise physical and gestural shifts of focus, which are then also reflected in the voice.

Having first tried playing a scene using very clear and deliberate physical and vocal signposting gestures, you can then try reducing the gestures so that the signposts are no more than shifts in your focus – slight inclinations of the head or changes in eyeline, accompanied as always by vocal shifts. By deliberately taking away the permission to make large hand gestures or to move towards the subject of the signpost, while continuing to shift your mental focus as the text instructs, you will begin to discover what the body actually *wants* to do, as your hands and body start to move of their own accord.

Once you arrive at the point where you can stop thinking about the signposting, allowing yourself to move and gesture on impulse, you should find that your body now understands its relationship with space, objective and text, and is able to signpost in its own way without needing to perform preset moves slavishly or mechanically. Very often you will discover that your body naturally chooses to signpost some things with more emphasis than others, so that while one signpost is achieved with a big physical gesture, another may become just a slight shift in focus and vocal tone.

The extent to which you retain the larger and more expansive gestures may also be dictated by your growing awareness of the character. Signposting can often play a key role in the process of your transformation into a character who, for personal or cultural reasons, may operate a more heightened and expressive physical/gestural vocabulary than your own. Working through signposting should therefore assist the process of building a character by enabling you to explore an aspect of your character's physical life within real moments of action and the pursuit of goals, rather than in a conjectural or generalised way.

7

Moving
Forward

As any good actor knows, you cannot walk into the performance space and act 'by numbers'; nor can you make assumptions about what the other actors are going to do. Every performance must be unique, and every performance must be about your reactions to real and present events happening *now*, not three weeks ago in rehearsal!

The Actioning exercises in this book are therefore emphatically not a set of instructions on how to build a formulaic or mechanical performance. Rather they are designed to help you *explore the different factors which converge in a moment of interaction*, and by exploring, to discover more about your character's relationship with:

- Other characters,

- The space,

- Their personal history,

- The world of the play.

When you take on a role within a scripted play, you embark upon the complex and difficult task of making your body, mind and emotions respond to stimuli as if you were someone other then yourself, living in circumstances other than your own. Most actors have powerful imaginations, or they couldn't be actors, but imagination alone is not enough. Actors also need *technique*, and by that I don't just mean finely tuned bodies and voices, but also the skill of sifting the text and exploring information and possibilities, so that each moment of performance will ultimately be readable, resonant, and completely distinguishable from the moments that precede and follow it.

You have to start from the assumption that every line or 'thought' in the text, whether or not the playwright consciously intended it, is in some way uniquely significant. There are no 'throwaway' lines – every single line of a text must contribute in some way to the overall story you are telling, because if it doesn't it is a waste of your time and that of your audience. Drama is not real life – it is a distillation of life, and your job as an actor is to make sure that not a single moment within that distillation is wasted.

Actioning, and the associated exercises contained in this book, constitute your interrogation, firstly of the text itself, and secondly of your own physical, psychological and emotional journey through a scene. By examining each aspect of that journey through a separate exercise, you can start to understand all the different pieces of information that in some way influence a moment of action, and how each might affect how your character thinks, feels and acts in that moment.

8

Interrogating the text and the character through these exercises does not mean you have to 'fix' your performance. What you are doing is asking questions and coming up with possible answers. These questions include all the basic Stanislavskian interrogations, such as 'what does my character *want*?' and 'what is his *obstacle*?', but also questions like 'what *effect* is my character trying to have on the other character at this point?' or 'how might my character *move* at this point, and why?' or 'what does this line of text *connect to* in my character's past?' or 'what does my character want the other character to *understand* on this line?'

The action verb is the 'junction box' to which all your questions and all your answers are connected. Each choice you make, whether about subtext, or physical moves, or resonator or signpost, must in some way connect back to and work with the original action verb. Anything that seems to contradict, or work against, the action verb is probably the wrong choice, unless, of course, you have chosen the wrong verb, in which case you should return to the text and choose a better one.

Engaging with this exploratory process will not and should not feel like performance. You will have moments of discovery, moments of exhilaration, possibly even moments of frustration and weariness. There may be some choices you make that will stay with you until the moment of performance, others that you simply let go. What you will actually be doing is giving yourself sufficient knowledge, understanding and body-learning, so that when you reach the point in rehearsal when you let go of your preparatory work and allow your impulses to take over, your work will not become random and generalised, but it will continue to be informed, to the last performance, by all of the questions that you have asked and the choices you have made.

8

There remains one final question: what if you are willing and able to use all the techniques and exercises associated with Actioning, yet the director and the other actors within your company do not subscribe to these techniques?

The answer to this is that you will rarely encounter 'ideal' working conditions, and your own training and 'toolbox' will often be unfamiliar to those who have not followed the same route into the profession. However, when you come up against such differences in practice, there will usually be several ways of dealing with this, as follows:

- Participate fully in whatever rehearsal technique the director employs, but use the Actioning technique within your own text work and preparation without necessarily drawing attention to the fact.

- Suggest aspects of the Actioning technique to the director and other actors, possibly as ways of conducting independent exploratory rehearsal work with your scene partners.

- Keep the Actioning technique and the associated exercises in reserve so that you have something to fall back on if the process you are following with the director and company does not ultimately provide the answers you are looking for.

As I have been at pains to emphasise throughout this book, the Actioning technique should *never* be used to construct a fixed performance. Actioning should always be seen as a way of sounding deeper, clearer and more contrasting 'notes' within an overall performance that remains at all times alive, reactive and instinctual. This being so, it should be possible, whatever process the director may be using, for you to bring those qualities into rehearsal and use them to stimulate a fuller investigation of character journeys and relationships.

8

Afterword

This book is designed to be read by student actors, by the people who train them and by working professionals. The techniques it describes can be utilised either as training processes or as tools to be used by actors and directors within the industry itself.

Actioning was invented as a way of keeping the actor in the 'intentional moment', maintaining focus on the other actor and playing the 'story' of the text, rather than becoming swamped in 'moods' or internal triggers that have little or nothing to do with the interaction.

Since the technique was developed in the 1970s, and most particularly in the last decade, those of us working in actor-training have noticed a significant change in the way student actors use their bodies. The advance of social media and the new habit of spending increasing amounts of time communicating through email, texting and other media, rather than through face-to-face encounters, has had a significant and palpable effect on the way the body is used.

In 1995, as part of a study of the implications of the new trend towards distance learning, Charlotte Gunawardena of the University of New Mexico wrote:

In traditional face-to-face interaction, besides what is actually verbalised, people exchange a range of non-verbal cues such as facial expression, direction of gaze, posture, dress and physical presence. These non-verbal cues perform two distinct functions. The first concerns itself directly with the passage of information from one individual to another; the second is the 'integrational aspects' of the communication process. Integrational aspects include all the physical manifestations of information exchange that keep the conversation going, regulate the interaction process, cross-reference particular messages to semantic meaning, and relate a particular context to larger contexts.

By the second decade of the twenty-first century, the phenomenon of 'distance' communication has pervaded every aspect of life, from friendships and relationships to working environments and political movements. The effect of this is that, consciously or unconsciously, many young people no longer find it necessary to employ the sign-systems of physical communication within their everyday encounters, even, and this is particularly significant, when they are actually *in* a face-to-face situation. More than ever before we see the eyes and facial muscles becoming the sole physical communicators, while the body hangs limply or engages in awkward 'displacement' activity, simply because it has no function within the encounter.

If our bodies are not 'alive', present and in relationship to other bodies, and if we do not practise this form of communication daily, we lose some of our capacity to feel empathy, to sense emotional change in another person and to pick up non-verbal signals that mediate between the words spoken and the meaning read. We all know how easy it is to misread an email – to impose our own interpretation of its tone because we have no signals telling us how to understand it. How then do we ensure that this ability to understand one another non-verbally does not become an inadvertent casualty of the new age of social media?

It is in this context that actor-trainers are setting out to turn the bodies of their students into clear and effective signifiers that can radiate meaning over long distances and allow unforced reactions to other actors to be processed, without self-censorship, into physical and vocal responses.

The most difficult task is teaching student actors to *think with their bodies*. Thought processed through the head alone can be detached and coldly analytical. Actors within the training process are anyway taught to free and support the breath, to release and inhabit the body, but all too often, within the rehearsal room, the 'artificiality' of speaking lines written by someone else within an imagined story whose ending we already know means that actors do not feel the need to engage the body or to activate the signifiers of physical presence and connection.

The Actioning technique, as I have explored it within this book, requires actors to go through a process of connecting thought and feeling to physical gesture and response. This process serves two purposes: on one level it can help actors to discover the physical 'story' of a scene; on another level it is an invaluable training tool that helps actors to explore the expressive potential of the body within the parameters of the text.

I believe that Actioning is an increasingly necessary tool for actors, and that through it they can find energy, range, variety and clarity of body and voice. In so doing, they may perhaps help to keep alive the communicational potentials of the body and learn to understand these things in themselves.

Also from Nick Hern Books

Actions: The Actors' Thesaurus is the essential guide for finding the right action verb in rehearsal. The most widely used and admired book for use in rehearsals today is now also available as an app for iOS devices.

Get the book for just £7.49 (25% off the RRP) plus free UK P&P when you use voucher code ACTIONING at www.nickhernbooks.co.uk

'*Actions: The Actors' Thesaurus* **is the perfect size to carry around, and I've found it invaluable in preparing for auditions as well as fleshing out a role.'** *Amazon reader review on the book*

'**Condenses all the usefulness of the book into a neat little app. Absolutely invaluable!'** *User review on the app*

www.actionsforactors.com
www.nickhernbooks.co.uk